God's 7 Steps To Financial Peace

By: Carolyn Wilde

Printed in the United States of America

2020 by Carolyn Wilde

Additional Books May Be Obtained

by Contacting:

Email: pcwilde@gulftel.com

Web site: newlifeinchristchurch.net

Paul or Carolyn Wilde

Post Office Box 1321

Foley, Alabama 36536

All Scriptures are taken from the King James Bible.

"Thy word is a lamp unto my feet, and a light unto my path." PSALM 119:105

"The entrance of thy words giveth light; it giveth understanding unto the simple." PSALM 119:130

"How sweet are thy words unto my taste! yea, sweeter than honey to my mouth!" PSALM 119:103

"For ever, O Lord, thy word is settled in heaven." PSALM 119:89

"Thy word is very pure: therefore thy servant loveth it." PSALM 119:140

"The words of the LORD are pure words: as silver tried in a furnace of earth, purified seven times. Thou shalt keep them, O LORD, thou shalt preserve them from this generation for ever." PSALM 12:6-7

TABLE OF CONTENTS

FINANCIAL PEACE ... 7

STEP 1: SIX DAYS YOU SHALL LABOR ... 13

STEP 2: THANKS FOR THE FISH! ... 35

STEP 3: THOU SHALT NOT COVET ... 47

STEP 4: FALSE BALANCES ... 73

STEP 5: A GIVING SPIRIT ... 87

STEP 6: GOD FIRST ... 109

STEP 7: GOD IS OUR SOURCE ... 125

CONCLUSION ... 143

A FINAL WORD ... 151

3 PRACTICAL STEPS TO GET OUT OF DEBT ... 155

FINANCIAL PEACE

What is financial peace of mind? Is there even such a thing?

Being rich does not bring financial peace of mind. Those who have money soon discover that they worry more about keeping it than they did about obtaining it.

Being poor does not bring financial peace of mind. The poor worry about their bills, and long for the big break that will make them rich.

One Man had financial peace of mind! He is Jesus Christ. He walked this earth with its financial systems and the unrest they bring. Yet, He alone lived above the love of money, the lust for money, the power of money, and the lack of money.

He followed **seven basic principles** in the Word of God. When we learn them, we may follow His example and live beyond and above the love of the filthy stuff that God describes as the root of *all* evil.

Money. It causes wars, ulcers, migraines, divorces, murders, thefts, prostitution, suicides ... and the list could go on and on. The Bible simply sums up all the problems it causes with this one conclusion: man's love for money is the root from which all evil grows.

The love of money reaches out and chokes the spiritual life out of all who are held in its deadly grip.

It is for this reason that the Bible contains more than 500 references to prayer and nearly 500 references to faith. Yet, there are more than 2,000 references to money and possessions! Sixteen, of the thirty-eight parables that Jesus told, deal with men and their money!

The poor strive for money, believing that it stands alone as their source of happiness.

Yet, the poor are not alone in their quest for it.

Money has a deceptive quality. The more man gets, the more man wants! There never seems to be quite enough to make one feel secure.

Many rich and powerful people have found that their accumulation of money does not give them the security they thought it would provide. Sleepless nights are just one of its side effects, as the wealthy lay awake worrying how best to invest it. They question the safety of the banks; if they have sufficient insurance; if their pensions will still be available when they need them; the security of their jobs; and even if the monetary system of their government will collapse.

Consider the following statements from the lips of multi-millionaires:

JOHN D. ROCKEFELLER was considered the richest person in modern history. At one time, he controlled 90% of the oil in the United States. His worth would be 409 billion dollars today. He said: *"I have made many millions, but they have brought me no happiness."*

W. H. VANDERBILT profited from the railroad industry. He said: **"The care of $200,000,000 is enough to kill anyone. There is no pleasure in it."**

JOHN JACOB ASTOR became wealthy by investing in real estate in New York City and in fur trade. At his death in 1848, he was named the richest man in the United States. His wealth today would be valued at 650 million dollars. He said: *"I am the most miserable man on earth."*

J. PAUL GETTY was named the world's richest private citizen in 1966. Oil was the source of his wealth. His worth today would be valued at 21 billion dollars. He said: *"What can I say? I only know I am desolate."*

HENRY Ford founded the *Ford Motor Company*. He said: *"I was happier when doing a mechanic's job."*

ANDREW Carnegie made his money in steel. During the last 18 years of his life, he gave away 350 million dollars, and he could afford it. His worth would be 65 billion dollars today. He said: ***"Millionaires seldom smile."***

These are testimonies from the wealthy, proof that money comes with no guarantee for happiness or security. Yet, multitudes of people down through the ages, both rich and poor, have given their hearts, souls, minds, and strength to obtain more of it.

Jesus said that man's heart, soul, mind, and strength should be filled with love for God. Jesus was the One who could claim this lifestyle confidently. His heart, soul, mind, strength, and life were wholly given to His Father.

Jesus was never once motivated by a love of money.

He put a thief in charge of His finances.

He did not even own a place to lay His head.

He gave of His services freely, both to the wealthy and to those in poverty.

He borrowed a donkey for His final ride into Jerusalem.

He was buried in a borrowed tomb.

He neither craved money, nor did He suffer for a lack of it.

He did not worry about it, nor did He suffer headaches, ulcers, or sleepless nights thinking about it.

He paid bills He did not owe.

He fed thousands of hungry people without charge.

He was the One Man who could not be controlled, bribed, or blackmailed by money. He neither lusted for it nor did He need it.

Why? Jesus **knew** and **lived by** the principles given by God, His Father.

If you are a follower of Jesus Christ, you can live by them too. These seven principles are clearly taught in the Bible. They are given to us by our Creator. When we follow each of these seven steps, we will ...

STOP
    WORRYING
        ABOUT
            MONEY!

STEP ONE

SIX DAYS YOU SHALL LABOR

We met John Zoller by accident ... or so we thought. We were driving to our home in Hart, Michigan, when we noticed a sign near Stony Lake that said "**JOHN ZOLLER**". We went on by, before realizing that we had heard a John Zoller preach on radio when we lived in Toledo, Ohio.

Could it be the same man who fearlessly preached God's Word?

We turned around, and hesitantly knocked on the door of the cozy, beautifully landscaped house. A man opened the door, and we asked if he was a radio preacher. He was! He heartily welcomed us inside, where we spent the afternoon listening to him relate stories of his incredible life of walking with the Lord.

He ministered to America's servicemen during World War II, beaming the gospel message around the world to them through radio.

He had fed thousands of hungry people in Flint, Michigan, during the Depression. He excitedly told us about our miracle-working God, who provided a daily supply of food in answer to his prayers.

He told us about the day in Chicago when he was surrounded by unsmiling men, who demanded that he come with them to meet their leader in a hotel room. He was ushered into a large room. Men sat around a huge table. At its head was Alphonse "Al" Capone, one of the most famous U.S. gangsters during the 1930s. John recognized him as the Chicago-based boss who was involved in illegal gambling, bootlegging illegal alcohol, and prostitution.

John didn't have to wonder long why he was brought before him. Capone demanded his share of John Zoller's radio profits! He handed him a contract, lacking only his signature. Signing it would deed Capone a percentage of all the income from his ministry.

John rose up to his full height of about five and a half feet and told Capone in a steely voice that he was entering territory he had better back out of fast, while he was still able!

"You dare not demand your share from God," Dr. Zoller stated. "I am a servant of God. I will not sign your contract, and you will **never** be given one penny of God's money through me. I am now leaving this room. I leave with this warning: do not **ever** threaten one of God's servants again!"

John then walked from the room, not knowing if he would live to leave the hotel.

He lived.

He did not hear from Al Capone or his men until the night much later, when he received a call from a pay telephone. The caller identified himself as one of Capone's men, who had been in the hotel room that day. He asked John to pray for him, saying he was marked for death and would be standing before God soon.

Sunday was his day to rest. Dr. Zoller was in his seventies when we met him. He told us that he had lived his life by dividing his days into three eight-hour segments: **(1) Work. (2) Rest. (3) Enjoy Life.** (John's enjoyment included eating, gardening, visiting, spending time with his family, and enjoying God's creation.)

He took us to his basement to see his work station. It was filled with books he had written and manuscripts that he hoped would one day become books. His shelves were lined with tapes of his sermons. His small studio, where he still recorded his daily radio programs, was also there. We had always noticed his beautifully tended garden when we passed by his house. It was proof that John worked!

One day we received a call with the news that John was in the hospital with heart trouble. We rushed to the hospital, expecting to see John, now in his eighties, forced into submitting to full-time rest. Instead, we found him propped up with pillows on a bed littered with papers. He explained in a weak, but firm voice that he was busy preparing literature for North Korea.

"My books are translated into the Korean language, and are then attached to balloons in South Korea near the border. When the wind is just right, the balloons are released. Spotters in North Korea shoot them down with bows and arrows, and my literature is then distributed."

We left his hospital room amazed. John has since passed into eternity, but his formula for life has remained with us. He lived a productive life, but took time out to smell the roses (including the ones he planted and grew) along the way.

We don't know if our Creator designed the twenty-four-hour day to be divided into three segments of work, sleep, and enjoyment, but it worked for John Zoller! We do know that God has set forth this principle for each week of your life: "Six days shalt thou labour, and do all thy work, but the seventh day is the sabbath of the Lord thy God: in it thou shalt not do any work, thou, nor thy son, nor thy daughter, thy manservant, nor thy maidservant, nor thy cattle, nor thy stranger that is within thy gates: for in six days the Lord made heaven and earth, the sea, and all that in them is, and rested the seventh day: wherefore the Lord blessed the sabbath day, and hallowed it." EXODUS 20:9-11

Jesus said of the sabbath day: **"The sabbath was made for man**, and not man for the sabbath." MARK 2:27

Sabbath is a word that simply means *rest*. Few use the sabbath as a day given by God to man to simply rest from his labors. One who works hard for six days would feel better emotionally, physically, mentally, and spiritually, if he rested one day a week. He would be more productive, not less, and accomplish more work in six days than he could have accomplished in seven!

One reason that men do not take the day of rest today is because he does not need it. He has not worked the other six days! Why would man need to rest one day, if he has not worked the other six days?

"**Six days shalt thou labour**, and **do all thy work**" is as much the commandment given by God as is the blessing of the day of rest! Yet, how many people in our day work diligently six days a week? We have become a pleasure-crazed people! Our energy is sapped by endless hours of texting, viewing television and computers, gaming, eating, drinking, sleeping, boating, partying ... and the list goes on and on.

Many men, who have faced a premature retirement from their jobs, have also faced a premature death from their inactivity. They have sought pleasure and rest seven days a week, and found no satisfaction in it.

Others have sought work with no pleasure, and have found no relaxation or enjoyment in it.

A few, like Dr. Zoller, have discovered that work, pleasure, and rest, combined in a disciplined week, brings satisfaction.

Work is not limited to a nine to five job. It can include sewing, gardening, helping a neighbor, repairing a child's bike, working in God's harvest field, patching an elderly neighbor's roof, sending a card to the discouraged, prayer, and visiting the sick. Work is defined as ***being engaged in meaningful activity directed to some purpose.***

Work may be hard or it may be easy. In either case, work is applying our energy toward a worthwhile result. Without work, we will wither and die.

Many paraplegics and invalids have found a meaningful life by discovering something that they can do to be productive. Some have developed their dormant artistic talents by drawing with a pencil held in their mouths. Others have engaged their minds, learning in a greater capacity than they would have been able to learn, if their bodies had not failed them.

Invalids like Charlotte Elliott ...

Charlotte lived a carefree life with her many friends, by painting their portraits and writing comical poems about them. She loved to hear people laugh and was known as the life of every party. She was 30 years old and, much to the dismay of her mother, had no plans to change her life of constant fun. Then her health failed, leaving her confined to her bed, unable to even lift either arm.

After a visit or two, her friends fled from her room, no longer recognizing their friend who had become bitter and overwhelmed with depression. As black despair engulfed her, she longed only for death.

She was left with no visitors and wanted none. She was enraged when her mother, despite her loud protests, ushered Dr. Caesar Malan, a renowned evangelist from Switzerland, into her room. Charlotte stubbornly faced the wall, refusing to even look at him. Yet, she could not escape his gentle voice. Finally, she turned her head to face him - and stared. There was a glow in his eyes - an unearthly light that literally enveloped her with love.

Dr. Malan continued to talk to her compassionately about his best Friend, Jesus Christ. He told her that a greater joy than she had ever known was hers for the asking. She wanted to believe him, but her heart and thoughts were filled with the blackness of rebellion and hatred. She had tried to free herself, for the sake of her exhausted parents. She had no strength left in her to make herself worthy to approach God for help.

Dr. Malan then spoke the words that not only changed Charlotte's life, but the lives of countless others. "Charlotte, you must come as a sinner to the Lamb of God that takes away the sin of the world ... **just as you are**."

"Are you telling me that Christ will receive me" Charlotte questioned, her eyes wide. *"Just as I am?"*

"Jesus shed his blood so He could receive you, Charlotte," Dr. Malan assured her.

Charlotte began to weep, as she prayed simply: "Oh, Jesus! Please be my Savior! Please be my Lord. Don't ever leave my side! Bring light to my dark heart!"

The Light that had glowed from Dr. Malan's eyes then banished the darkness in her black heart. Her days of despair changed into days of unspeakable joy. She continued to endure pain, overpowering weakness, and exhaustion. Yet, her depression was miraculously forever gone. Charlotte's room once again filled with visitors. She spoke to each one of them about Jesus. "His grace surrounds me! His voice continually bids me to be happy and holy in His service - *just where I am.*"

One night, Charlotte woke suddenly, feeling her Savior's Presence surrounding her. She managed to whisper just two words: "**My Lord**".

Charlotte heard Christ's tender, yet commanding voice, as He spoke to her heart. **"Charlotte. Follow Me."**

How she wished she could obey Him. Yet, she knew she could not give the answer He wanted to hear. She finally had the courage to whisper: "Lord, I cannot follow You. Do you not see me? Do you want an invalid to follow You? I cannot walk! I have been confined to this bed for seventeen years! You will need to find a healthy person to follow You. I am worthless to You ... and to everyone!"

The Lord's Presence did not leave with her refusal. Instead, she felt His eyes looking even deeper into her soul. She waited for His next words. There were none.

He simply waited, until she breathed out the words: "I will follow You, my Lord." She expected Him to raise her from her bed. He didn't. A short time later, in the early morning hours, Charlotte moved her hand enough to grasp her paper and pen. Perhaps if she wrote of her salvation, someone could be helped. Slowly, Charlotte Elliott began to write. You may have heard her words, for they have been put to music and sung throughout the world.

Just as I am, without one plea
But that Thy blood was shed for me,
And that Thou bidd'st me come to Thee,
O Lamb of God, I come!   I come!

Just as I am, and waiting not
To rid my soul of one dark blot
To Thee whose blood can cleanse each spot,
O Lamb of God, I come!   I come!

Just as I am, tho tossed about
With many a conflict, many a doubt,
Fightings and fears within, without,
O Lamb of God, I come!   I Come!

Just as I am, Thou wilt receive,
Wilt welcome, pardon, cleanse, relieve;
Because Thy promise I believe,
O Lamb of God, I come!   I come!

As Charlotte's song gave hope to the weary, the oppressed, and the brokenhearted, many responded by answering the call to simply come to Christ ... ***just as they were***. Thousands of letters from many nations poured into the home where Charlotte lay.

Charlotte spent 52 years of her life confined to her bed. Yet, still today, the heartfelt invitation from a helpless soul on a lonely bed is still calling souls to Jesus.

Charlotte went to be with her Savior in 1871. Revelation 14:13 tells us about those who die in the Lord and rest from their labors - and their works follow them. The work that Charlotte did as an invalid is still following her.

Then there was John Wesley ...

John Wesley was a disciplined, productive preacher. He traveled 250,000 miles on horseback, averaging twenty miles a day for forty years! He preached 40,000 sermons! He produced 400 books! He knew ten languages!

At eighty-three years of age, he was annoyed that he could not write more than fifteen hours a day without hurting his eyes.

At eighty-six years of age, he was ashamed that he could no longer preach more than twice a day!

He complained in his diary that he had an increasing tendency to lie in bed until 5:30 in the morning!

John Wesley probably did not smell many roses, but he surely did his share of work! He also kept one day set apart for his day of rest.

If you are not engaged in work six days a week, you are not following the principle of God. If you are lazy, unwilling to work, expecting your family or your government to provide for you, hoping to get ahead by winning the lottery or by the death of an unknown rich uncle, you will never have peace of mind.

God's Word warns: "Wealth gotten by vanity shall be diminished: but he that gathereth by labour shall increase." PROVERBS 13:11

The Bible says much about work. Even before Adam's fall in the Garden of Eden, the Scriptures record that God put Adam "...into the garden of Eden to dress it and to keep it." GENESIS 2:15

After Adam's fall, God made man's work more difficult. He told Adam: "...cursed is the ground for thy sake; in sorrow shalt thou eat of it all the days of thy life; thorns also and thistles shall it bring forth to thee; and thou shalt eat the herb of the field; in the sweat of thy face shalt thou eat bread, till thou return unto the ground..." GENESIS 3:17-19

Work was not the curse given to man. God Himself worked before man's fall, when He created the world. Genesis 2:2-3 says, "... on the seventh day God ended **his work** which he had made; and he rested on the seventh day from all **his work** which he had made. And God blessed the seventh day, and sanctified it: because that in it he had rested from **all his work** which God created and made."

God worked. He also gave work and the responsibility of the upkeep of the garden to Adam before the fall of man.

The curse did not bring work. The curse brought work under adverse conditions ... thorns, thistles, potato bugs, tomato worms, locusts, termites, and diseases that would destroy the work of man almost as fast as it got done.

Work was here before the fall, and man will still be involved in work when our present age ends. Paul said to the saints at Corinth: "Do ye not know that the saints shall judge the world? Know ye not that we shall judge angels?" I CORINTHIANS 6:2-3

Ask any judge if he considers his job to be work!

After the return of Jesus Christ, God's Word says that those who have come triumphantly out of great tribulation "are before the throne of God and *serve him day and night* in his temple. And there shall be no more curse; but the throne of God and of the Lamb shall be in it; and **his servants** shall serve him!" REVELATION 7:15 AND 22:3

Ask any servant if his service is work!

Revelation 5:9-10 tells us of the ones who have been redeemed by the blood of Jesus "... out of every kindred, and tongue, and people, and nation; and has made us unto our God kings and priests: and we shall **reign** on the earth!"

Ask any king or priest if he considers his various responsibilities work!

Until the fall and curse of man, there was pleasure in work. With the curse came the destroyer, who takes pleasure in devouring man's labors and making his work an endless cycle with little lasting accomplishment. Until the day the destroyer is bound, work and sweat will go on, hand in hand.

God did not create man to be idle. A diligent person is one who is active, busy, and industrious.

A slothful person is one who is idle and lazy. God's Word tells us that "the hand of the diligent shall bear rule: but the slothful shall be under tribute. He also that is slothful in his work is brother to him that is a great waster. Slothfulness casteth into a deep sleep; and an idle soul shall suffer hunger."

"The sluggard will not plow by reason of the cold; therefore shall he beg in harvest, and have nothing. Love not sleep, lest thou come to poverty; open thine eyes, and thou shalt be satisfied with bread. The desire of the slothful killeth him; for his hands refuse to labour. For the drunkard and the glutton shall come to poverty: and drowsiness shall clothe a man with rags."

"As the door turneth upon his hinges, so doth the slothful upon his bed. I went by the field of the slothful, and by the vineyard of the man void of understanding; and, lo, it was all grown over with thorns, and nettles had covered the face thereof, and the stone wall thereof was broken down. Then I saw, and considered it well: I looked upon it, and received instruction. Yet a little sleep, a little slumber, a little folding of the hands to sleep: so shall thy poverty come as one that travelleth; and thy want as an armed man." PROVERBS 12:24 + 18:9 + 19:15 + 20:4 & 13 + 21:25 +23:21 + 26:14 & 30-34

Paul wrote Timothy: "This we commanded you, that if any **would not work**, neither should he eat. For we hear that there are some which walk among you disorderly, **working not at all**, but are busybodies. Now them that are such we command and exhort by our Lord Jesus Christ, that with quietness they **work**, and eat their own bread." II THESSALONIANS 3:10-12

God warns: "If any provide not for his own, and specially for those of his own house, he hath denied the faith, and is worse than an infidel." I TIMOTHY 5:8

Included in the description of a virtuous woman is this characteristic: "She worketh willingly with her hands." PROVERBS 31:13

A sluggard is a person who is habitually lazy and idle. Solomon said: "Go to the ant, thou sluggard; consider her ways, and be wise: which having no guide, overseer, or ruler, provideth her meat in the summer, and gathereth her food in the harvest. How long wilt thou sleep, O sluggard? When wilt thou arise out of thy sleep? Yet a little sleep, a little slumber, a little folding of the hands to sleep: so shall thy poverty come ..." PROVERBS 6:6-11

"The soul of the sluggard desireth, and hath nothing: but the soul of the diligent shall be made fat." PROVERBS 13:4

One wise man said: "The only place where success comes before work is in the dictionary!"

When Jesus sent out seven of His disciples, He told them: "The **labourer** is worthy of his hire."   LUKE 10:7

Jesus sent His disciples out to work!   Jesus did not send His disciples out to do something He Himself was not willing to do. Jesus worked! John wrote about some of the work that Jesus did, and then concluded his book with this startling statement: "And there are also many other things which Jesus did, the which, if they should be written every one, I suppose that even the world itself could not contain the books that should be written!"   JOHN 21:25

Matthew 9:35-37 records of Him: "Jesus went about all the cities and villages, **teaching** in their synagogues, and **preaching** the gospel of the kingdom, and **healing** every sickness and every disease among the people. But when he saw the multitudes, he was moved with compassion on them ... then saith he unto his disciples, The harvest truly is plenteous, but the *labourers* are few; pray ye therefore the Lord of the harvest, that he will send forth **labourers** into his harvest."

Jesus was constantly mobbed with people, begging for His touch. There were endless lines of sick people, possessed people, and hungry people. There were disciples to train and multitudes to teach. However, even though there was so much for Jesus to do and He was the only Son of God who could do the job, He still took time to rest, and instructed His disciples to do so. "Come ye yourselves apart into a desert place, and rest a while," Jesus told them.

Mark adds: "... for there were many coming and going, and they had no leisure so much as to eat. And they departed into a desert place by ship privately." MARK 6:31-32

Jesus worked while on earth and He works yet today.

When He was only twelve years old, He said: "I must be about my Father's business." LUKE 2:49

Years later, He said: "I must work the works of him that sent me." JOHN 9:4

Jesus is not idle in heaven now. Before His ascension, He gave us a glimpse of what He would be doing, for He said: "I go to prepare a place for you." JOHN 14:2

Paul told us that, even now, Jesus "... maketh intercession for us." ROMANS 8:34

God does not ask us to do something that He does not do Himself. God started this earth with the principle of six days of work, followed by a day of rest. God still works today. Aren't you glad that you can call upon Him in your time of trouble, and you can know that He is wide awake and ready to help you?

If God worked six days ... *how much more should we?*

If God rested one day after working six ... *how much more should we?*

If Jesus worked while on earth ... *how much more should we?*

If Jesus took time to rest ... *how much more should we?*

If you are a workaholic, who does not take time for a day of rest each week, you will not find peace of mind. God gave you one day out of seven to rest. Take it. Your other six days will not only be more productive, they will be far more satisfying, and you will be better equipped to face the pressures that come your way.

God's principle is:

Work six days.

Rest one day.

God even commanded His people to follow this principle with the earth itself. He told Moses, on Mount Sinai: "Six years thou shalt sow thy field, and six years thou shalt prune thy vineyard, and gather in the fruit thereof; but *in the seventh year shall be a sabbath of rest unto the land*, a sabbath for the Lord: thou shalt neither sow thy field, nor prune thy vineyard. That which groweth of its own accord of thy harvest thou shalt not reap, neither gather the grapes of thy vine undressed: for it is a year of *rest unto the land*." LEVITICUS 25:3-5

This principle is embedded in all of God's creation. If we do not follow it, we will not have peace of mind.

If you work seven days a week, the daily pressures will eventually catch up with you and break you.

If we do not work, we will have guilt feelings that will rob us of peace of mind. If our bodies are incapacitated, we can still use our minds!

If you do not know how to be productive, ask God for wisdom. He has a promise for you in James 1:5: "If any of you lack wisdom, let him ask of God, that giveth to all men liberally, and upbraideth not; and it shall be given him. But let him ask in faith, nothing wavering. For he that wavereth is like a wave of the sea driven with the wind and tossed. For let not that man think that he shall receive any thing of the Lord."

The promise is not: "If any of you lack riches, let him ask of God, that giveth to all men liberally."

Riches will not give you financial peace of mind.

Following all seven of God's principles will, and one of them is simply ...

**Work six days a week.
Rest one day a week.**

And remember: "Poverty and shame shall be to him that refuseth instruction: but he that regardeth reproof shall be honoured." PROVERBS 13:18

Before we leave Step 1, let's obey our Lord's counsel to **"go to the ant; consider her ways**, and be wise: which having no guide, overseer, or ruler, provideth her meat in the summer, and gathereth her food in the harvest."

ANTS

An ant can carry up to 27 times its own weight without even puffing! This would be equivalent to a 148-pound person not just lifting - but **_carrying_** - 4,000 pounds, the weight of a small SUV!

(Note: The Lord instructs us in Galatians 6:2: "Bear ye one another's burdens, and so fulfil the law of Christ."

If an ant can carry monstrous burdens, the Lord can surely give His children the strength to lift the burdens of people in need!)

An ant cooperates with its fellow ants for the good of the whole ant colony. Colonies vary in size from a dozen to thousands upon thousands of ants. Each colony is divided into these three castes:

(1) The queen ant is responsible for founding a new colony and laying eggs that produce new ants to keep the colony going. She tunnels underground to make a nest, and all alone, seals herself into her tunnel to lay her eggs.

(2) The winged male ants fertilize the queen's eggs. When their task is finished, they immediately die.

(3) The female worker ants work - and work - and work! They dig tunnels and maintain them. They clean, groom, and feed each other. They collect food and tend to the needs of all the baby ants. They hunt. They even form armies to defend their colony against intruders!

Ants have a stomach that is divided into two parts. One part (the crop) is a temporary food storage place for the entire colony. The other part is each ant's personal supply of food. When an ant finds food, it chews it up and dissolves it into a liquid. Most of this liquid food goes into the crop. Only a tiny bit goes into the other part, for its own use. Back at the colony, the ant with the full crop helps feed the others!

Some ants are farmers.

The leaf-cutting ants of Louisiana and Texas take leaves into their underground nests and grow a special fungus, or kind of mushroom, on them.

Other ants are dairy farmers. They tend aphids, in the same way that dairy farmers tend cows. Aphids are tiny insects that overfeed on plant juices. As ants softly stroke the backs of the aphids with their antennae, tiny drops of honeydew come out. The industrious ants then store them in their crops.

Harvester ants fill special storerooms in their mounds with great quantities of seeds that they have gathered. They then mill the seeds by crushing them with their strong jaws. The end product of their chewing is a "bread" that feeds all the ants in the colony. The seeds that start to sprout, before they can be chewed, are carried away from the ant mound and left to grow.

Honey ants feed on honeydew from other insects, nectar from flowers, and other plant juices. Food is not always readily available in the dry plains and deserts of the western United States, where these ants live. So, they store up food for the hard times. Their storage pantry is in other ants! During good times, these special ants are fed until they can hardly move. Then they hang from the ceiling of the nest until their food is needed. During the lean times, they are tapped for food to keep the colony alive. They become living honeypots!

When we "look to the ants and consider them" we quickly learn why our Creator's counsel to a lazy man is: "Go to the ant, thou sluggard!"

STEP TWO

THANKS FOR THE FISH!

Jesus demonstrated one of the most valuable principles in the Scriptures concerning financial peace of mind.

Matthew records this beautiful principle: "And Jesus departed ... and came nigh unto the sea of Galilee; and went up into a mountain, and sat down there. And great multitudes came unto him, having with them those that were lame, blind, dumb, maimed, and many others, and cast them down at Jesus' feet; and he healed them: insomuch that the multitude wondered, when they saw the dumb to speak, the maimed to be whole, the lame to walk, and the blind to see: and they glorified the God of Israel.

"Then Jesus called his disciples unto him, and said, I have compassion on the multitude, because they continue with me now three days, and have nothing to eat: and I will not send them away fasting, lest they faint in the way. And his disciples say unto him, Whence should we have so much bread in the wilderness, as to fill so great a multitude?

"And Jesus saith unto them, How many loaves have ye? And they said, Seven, and a few little fishes. And he commanded the multitude to sit down on the ground. And he took the seven loaves and the fishes, and **gave thanks**, and brake them, and gave to his disciples, and the disciples to the multitude. And they did all eat, and were filled: and they took up of the broken meat that was left seven baskets full. And they that did eat were four thousand men, beside women and children." MATTHEW 15:29-38

Jesus had ministered until He was weary. When one woman was healed by simply touching the hem of His garment, He said that virtue (strength), had left His body. He ministered daily to the masses, leaving his own body drained. He retreated to a mountain to rest, but the multitudes, carrying their invalids and leading their blind, followed Him. They lay their burdens at Jesus' feet, pleading with Him to give them all just a touch of His power.

His compassion overcame His weariness, as Jesus ministered to all who came to Him for His healing touch. He gave His strength unreservedly for three days.

Now they were ready to leave. Their sick were healed; their blind saw; their deaf heard; and their lame leaped and danced. Jesus tenderly looked at them, realizing that they had one more unfulfilled need. They were hungry. He shared their need for food and strength for their journey home with His disciples.

They looked around them and saw nothing but wilderness. There were no super markets, no fast food restaurants ... no food available anywhere. They looked at the thousands of hungry people. Then they looked at Jesus. Could He seriously be considering feeding these people?

Apparently, He was. He gave them a new mission, sending them to search among the crowd for food. They returned to Him, carrying a mere seven loaves of bread and a few little fishes.

"And He took the seven loaves and the fishes, and **gave thanks** ..."

Think about this for a moment. Jesus did not have enough food to feed even Himself and His own disciples, let alone four-thousand men and their wives and children!

He looked at the thousands of hungry people. Then He looked at the meager food that was given to Him.

Jesus then did what no mere man would have done.

He gave thanks for the little that He had!

Jesus demonstrated a tremendous principle in the Word of God!

He gave thanks for what was clearly not enough for the need.

He did not complain about what He did not have!

The crowd was not only filled, but there were leftovers at the end of their meal!

John told us about another time; another place; and another hungry multitude. This time, Jesus had five barley loaves and only two small fishes. This time, there were about five-thousand hungry men.

"And Jesus took the loaves; and **when He had given thanks** ..."

John finished recording the miracle, and began telling about the events of the next day. He wrote: "Howbeit there came other boats from Tiberias nigh unto the place where they did eat bread, **after that the Lord had given thanks**." JOHN 6:1-3 & 23

Jesus made a lasting impression on John. He thanked His Father for His provisions, even though they were, to the natural eye, far short of meeting the need.

If we will begin to thank God for what He has given us, *then* He will bless it and multiply it!

Do you do this?

When you receive your paycheck and look at the few dollars remaining after your taxes have been deducted, and then look at the pile of bills on the desk ... do you thank your Father in heaven for the money you *do* have? Or do you grumble and complain about the amount you *do not* have to cover your bills?

The children of Israel, led by Moses from Egypt into the land promised to them, were miraculously sustained by their Creator. Food literally fell from the heavens.

The Bible says: "... when the dew that lay was gone up, behold, upon the face of the wilderness there lay a small round thing, as small as the hoar frost on the ground. And when the children of Israel saw it, they said one to another,

It is manna: for they wist not what it was. And Moses said unto them, This is the bread which the Lord hath given you to eat!" EXODUS 16:14-15

Manna simply means *What is this?   It is a portion!*

The children of Israel had not planted it, watered it, harvested it, or purchased it. They simply went and picked it up. They gathered a daily supply five days a week, and on the sixth day, they gathered enough for two days.

Numbers 11:8 tells us that "... the people went about, and gathered it, and ground it in mills, or beat it in a mortar, and baked it in pans, and made cakes of it: and the taste of it was as the taste of fresh oil."

Exodus 16:31 describes manna as "coriander seed, white; and the taste of it was like wafers made with honey."

Psalm 78:23-25 tells us that God "... opened the doors of heaven, and had rained down manna upon them to eat, and had given them of the corn of heaven. Man did eat angels' food: he sent them meat to the full!"

How could these people fail to be thankful?

God had delivered them from slave labor!

He gave them miraculous victories over their cruel masters!

He was leading them to a land He promised them!

He blessed them with one of history's most compassionate leaders!

He quenched their thirst with water from a dry rock!

He poured the food of angels down from the heavens!

Yet, they were still not satisfied.   They were not thankful for their blessings.

Listen to their whines: "... Who shall give us flesh to eat? We remember the fish, which we did eat in Egypt freely; the cucumbers, and the melons, and the leeks, and the onions, and the garlick: but now our soul is dried away: there is nothing at all, beside this manna, before our eyes!" NUMBERS 11:4-6

Before we judge them too harshly, let us put ourselves in their place.

We may have loved manna ... *at first*.

We ate it on Monday for breakfast.

We opened our lunch box at school or work, and found manna.

We returned home, hoping for a good meal, but tried to hide our disappointment when we saw the casserole of manna on the table.

Tuesday's menu was manna.

Wednesday's menu was manna.

Thursday's menu was manna.

Friday's menu was manna.

Saturday's menu - surely there would be something other than manna on the Sabbath - but no. We were served manna.

There was no need to even check Sunday's menu. We would already know what it would be ... more manna.

Wives, mothers, and chefs had faithfully prepared the manna in many different ways. But the food never varied.

Week after week, month after month, year after year, we would eat manna.

Would *you* thank God for the manna?

Or would you murmur and complain, voicing your longing for a good hamburger, hot dog, french fries, baked potato, or steak?

Then there was the water out of a rock. God did not pour a soft drink, fruit juice, or a chocolate milk shake out of the rock. He did not turn the rock into a huge coffee urn each morning, satisfying man's longing for a fresh, hot cup of coffee to start their day. Instead, good old plain water was served with their manna.

Meal after meal ... manna and water.
Day after day ... manna and water.
Year after year ... Manna and water.

Yes, they complained. Yes, they grumbled. Yes, they longed for a variation of food. Just a little onion and garlick for flavoring would have helped! God finally sickened of their complaints, and sent flocks of quails for them to eat. Sadly, by then their murmuring, complaining, and grumbling had become a habit.

They had become a bitter, unthankful people.

How different they were from Jesus!

He had thousands of unexpected guests for dinner and had nothing but a little food that could satisfy two or three guests at the most. Yet, Jesus was so thankful for what He did have, that He took time to lift His eyes toward the heavens and say: "Thank You, Father, for this food You have provided for Me!"

Jesus showed us His heart of thankfulness at what we call the Last Supper. Before serving bread to His disciples, He **thanked His Father** for it. Then He said to them: "This is my body which is given for you." Before serving them the cup, He again thanked His Father for it. Then He told them: "This is my blood of the new testament, which is shed for many for the remission of sins." LUKE 22:19 + MATTHEW 26:27-28

Jesus thanked His Father for His body that would be broken for us!

Jesus thanked His Father for His blood that would be shed for us!

He then began His lonely trip to Gethsemane, the cross, and the tomb.

WHAT A WONDERFUL SAVIOR WE HAVE!

Now would be a good time to pause reading and **thank your Father** for sending His Son to save us!

Now would be a good time to **thank Jesus** for giving His body and shedding His blood to save us!

Men stood at the foot of the cross as Jesus died, mocking Him with these words: "He saved others; let him save himself, if he be Christ, the chosen of God!" LUKE 23:35

They spoke truth. If Christ had listened to the mockers, He would have saved Himself. Instead, our precious Savior chose to save others, rather than to save Himself. Jesus would not save Himself, for He was saving us.

Jesus laid down His life for us - **with a thankful heart**.

Paul, the apostle of Jesus, wrote to young Timothy concerning the condition of the people living in the last days. One of their identifying traits was that they would be unthankful. (SEE II TIMOTHY 3:1-2.)

Are we an unthankful people?

Are we thankful for the car we have? Or do we grumble because it does not have the latest electronic perks?

Are we thankful for the house we have? Or do we complain because it does not have more rooms?

Do we thank God for the clothes and shoes we have? Or do we gripe because they are not the current name brand?

Are we thankful for the job we have? Or do we murmur because we do not have all the benefits we think we are entitled to?

Are we thankful for the money to pay the bills we can pay? Or are we too busy complaining about the ones we can't pay?

No one enjoys keeping company with a bitter person who complains all the time. *Neither does God*.

As long as we repeat the mistake God's children of Israel made, complaining, murmuring, and grumbling constantly about God's provisions and always longing for something different, newer, better or more, God's blessings will not be upon us.

Would we continue to give a gift to someone each year for his birthday, if he never responded with a thank you? Would we want to give more to him, if his only comment was a complaint? What parent would enjoy giving his child a gift, if he consistently discarded it, complaining that he wanted a better gift?

God's Word, referring to the children of Israel, warns us: "Neither murmur ye, as some of them also murmured, and were destroyed of the destroyer. Now all these things happened unto them for ensamples: and they are written for our admonition, upon whom the ends of the world are come." I CORINTHIANS 10:10-11

Romans 1:21 says: "...when they knew God, they glorified him not as God, *neither were thankful*; but became vain in their imaginations, and their foolish heart was darkened."

God tells us that we should be "... *giving thanks always for all things* unto God and the Father in the name of our Lord Jesus Christ." EPHESIANS 5:20

Hebrews 13:15 instructs us to "... offer the sacrifice of praise to God continually, that is, the fruit of *our lips giving thanks to His name*."

Jesus was especially pleased with the one leper who returned to Him to thank Him for his healing. We read this story in Luke 17:15-17: "And one of them, when he saw that he was healed, turned back, and with a loud voice glorified God, and fell down on his face at his feet, **giving him thanks** ... And Jesus answering said, Were there not ten cleansed? but where are the nine?"

Where were the nine, who could not even turn around and thank their Healer?

God saw a bitter, complaining spirit in His children in the wilderness. We hear His displeasure when we listen to His sentence of judgment.

"How long shall I bear with this evil congregation, which murmur against me? I have heard the murmurings of the children of Israel, which they murmur against me. Say unto them, As truly as I live, saith the Lord, as ye have spoken in mine ears, so will I do to you: your carcases shall fall in this wilderness; and all that were numbered of you, according to your whole number, from twenty years old and upward which have murmured against me." NUMBERS 14:27-29

Murmurs are *continuous complaints*.

God has not changed. He wants to bless His people today. Yet, He will still pass over the one with a bitter, complaining spirit and seek the one who has a thankful heart.

Listen to His promise in II Chronicles 16:9: "For the eyes of the Lord run to and fro throughout the whole earth, to shew himself strong in the behalf of them whose heart is perfect toward him."

Be thankful for *everything* that God has given you, even when it does not seem enough to meet your need.

When God sees your thankful heart, He will multiply what He has given you, and your every need will be met!

STEP THREE

THOU SHALT NOT COVET

It may shock you to realize what a typical Western family would need to give up in order to adopt the lifestyle of a typical family living among our billion hungry neighbors.

Robert Heilbroner, an economist, has itemized the abandoned "luxuries".

We begin by invading the house of our imaginary family to strip it of its furniture. Everything goes: beds, chairs, tables, the television set, lamps. We will leave the family with a few old blankets, a kitchen table, and a wooden chair. Along with the bedroom furniture, the clothes will go. Each member of the family may keep his oldest suit or dress and one shirt or blouse in his wardrobe. We will permit one pair of shoes for the head of the family, but no shoes for the wife or the children.

We then move to the kitchen. The appliances have already been taken away, so we will turn to the cupboards. The box of matches may stay, along with a small bag of flour, some sugar, and some salt. A few moldy potatoes must be rescued from the garbage can, for they will provide much of today's main meal. We will leave a handful of onions and a dish of dried beans. The rest must be removed: the meat, the fresh vegetables, the canned goods, the crackers, and the candy.

The house has been stripped.

The bathroom has been dismantled.

The running water has been shut off.

The electric wires have been removed.

Next, we take away the house itself.

The family will move to the toolshed.

Communication must go next. There will be no books, magazines, computers, or phones.

They will not be missed, since we must take away our family's literacy as well. We will allow one radio in our shanty town.

All government services must go. There will be no more mailmen or firemen. There is a school, but it is three miles away and consists of only two classrooms.

There are, of course, no hospitals or doctors nearby. The nearest clinic is ten miles away and it is tended by one midwife. It can be reached by bicycle, provided the family has a bicycle as its sole means of transportation, which is unlikely.

Finally, the money must go. We will allow our family a cash hoard of $5.00.

How many people confront this kind of grinding poverty today? The estimate is at least one billion.

We scoff when we hear that foreigners believe that all Americans are rich. However, in the light of the above comparison, are we not wealthy?

God's Word says: "... godliness with contentment is great gain. For we brought nothing into this world, and it is certain we can carry nothing out. And having food and raiment let us be therewith content. But ***they that will be rich*** fall into temptation and a snare, and into many foolish and hurtful lusts, which drown men in destruction and perdition. For **the <u>love</u> of money is the root of <u>all</u> evil**: which while some coveted after, they have erred from the faith, and pierced themselves through with many sorrows." I TIMOTHY 6:6-10

It is not the money that is the root of all evil! It is man's love for it!

It is all ***who will be rich*** (*who desire to be rich*) who are snared in its net of greed.

How many people do you know who are absolutely content with what they have?

Are not most of your neighbors, friends, and relatives striving to obtain more? Most want just one more piece of furniture, one more suit, a newer car, a better house, a raise in pay, more money in the bank for retirement, or a larger insurance policy.

Job was the richest man in the east. Then, in just one dark day, all his wealth vanished. Job lost 7,000 sheep, 3,000 camels, 500 yoke of oxen, 500 she asses, many servants, his seven sons, and his three daughters.

Job fell to the ground. *We would too.*

But how many of us would fall to the ground ... *and worship God?* "Job arose ... and fell down upon the ground, and *worshipped."*

We hear his cry echoing down the ages: "... naked came I out of my mother's womb, and naked shall I return thither: the Lord gave, and the Lord hath taken away; blessed be the name of the Lord!" JOB 1:20-21

Would you worship God on the day you were stripped of your possessions, your employees, and every one of your children?

The apostle Paul said that he had experienced hunger, thirst, cold, nakedness, prison sentences, three shipwrecks, beatings, a stoning, being robbed, weariness, and pain. Then he added these triumphant words: "Not that I speak in respect of want: for I have learned, in whatsoever state I am, therewith to be content. I know both how to be abased, and I know how to abound: every where and in all things I am instructed both to be full and to be hungry, both to abound and to suffer need." PHILIPPIANS 4:11-12

Job's and Paul's contentment did not depend on their abundance of possessions.

They had learned the truth of Jesus' warning: "Take heed, and beware of covetousness: for a man's life consisteth not in the abundance of the things which he possesseth." LUKE 12:15

Are you just as contented when you have nothing, as when you have much of this world's goods?

Does your happiness depend on whether or not you have money in your wallet?

Jesus warned us to beware of covetousness.

What is this thing called covetousness?

The dictionary defines covetousness as ***an excessive desire for things; greed.*** However, God's definition is shocking:

"Mortify *(kill)* therefore your members which are upon the earth; fornication, uncleanness, inordinate affection, evil concupiscence, and **covetousness**, **which is idolatry**: for which things' sake the wrath of God cometh on the children of disobedience: for this ye know, that no whoremonger, nor unclean person, nor **covetous man**, **who is an idolater**, hath any inheritance in the kingdom of Christ and of God. Let no man deceive you with vain words: for because of these things cometh the wrath of God upon the children of disobedience. Be not ye therefore partakers with them." COLOSSIANS 3:5-6 AND EPHESIANS 5:5-7

If God views covetousness as idolatry (as indeed He does), America is the most idolatrous country on earth! We think of idolatry as a sin of heathen countries, picturing unenlightened worshipers kneeling before ugly gold idols.

But God labels idolatry covetousness. Our excessive greed for more makes us the idolaters, according to the Word of God. Are we not all guilty?

We are born into sin, and it is apparent from our childhood that covetousness is part of our Adamic nature.

It is fed by our affluent society. The toy boxes overflow, and stuffed animals line nursery walls. As a child watches animated shows, he views endless commercials that appeal to his covetous nature and appetites.

Christmas arrives, and any reminder of Jesus' birth is buried under mountains of presents. Yet, we never have quite enough.

The child grows. The boy wants a motor scooter. The girl wants clothes. They both want the newest electronic devices. And the lists of desires go on - and on - and on.

It is time for college. A stylish wardrobe and a car is needed.

A wedding is planned. Thousands of dollars are spent to impress the guests during a twenty-minute ceremony.

The marriage follows. The groom and his bride expect to begin their new lives in a home equipped with all the luxuries that their parents worked years to acquire. The result is debt. Credit card balances grow out of control.

Inevitably, the bills come in, and with them, the shock of their total debt. Panic ensues, yet they lust for more and better. So they continue to charge. They are forced to find extra jobs.

A baby is conceived. Can they afford a child? How will they survive the extra expenses? How can they afford day care? Abortion is the easy answer for nearly twenty percent of the pregnancies in America.

It all begins with covetousness. It ends with murdering a precious baby.

Over 60 million babies have been aborted since the United States legalized this act of murder in 1973.

Perhaps the parents' decision is to have the baby. Those with covetous hearts are unwilling to give up their lust for more possessions. Financial pressures soon begin to crush them. The husband has two jobs. The wife is wearily juggling her time with a job, housekeeping, cooking, and the added responsibility of the baby.

The baby is often raised by indifferent babysitters or dropped off at the nearest day care facility. The mother's income must continue.

The load on both parents is too much. Fights come easily, because of the combined pressures of overwork, pressures, and exhaustion.

There is no time for a picnic, a day spent together, a walk on the beach, or church attendance. There is no time for God or one another. The marriage deteriorates a little more each day, until it finally ends in a bitter divorce. The number one cause of failed marriages is financial pressure, caused by covetousness. Divorce offers no answer, as expenses continue and even multiply. Two houses must be maintained. Child support must be paid.

It all begins with that deadly sin called covetousness. It is little wonder that God warned: "He that is greedy of gain troubleth his own house." PROVERBS 15:27

We would do well to heed these Proverbs: "Better is little with the fear of the Lord than great treasure and trouble therewith. Better is a dinner of herbs where love is, than a stalled ox and hatred therewith." PROVERBS 15:16-17

A covetous man, who has heaped treasure upon his family, is generally well respected in his community. Yet, God warns: "For the wicked boasteth of his heart's desire, and blesseth the covetous, whom the Lord abhorreth." PSALM 10:3

Paul looked ahead to our generation and wrote this prophecy: "In the last days perilous times shall come. For men shall be lovers of their own selves, **covetous**, boasters, proud." II TIMOTHY 3:1-2

The average amount of personal debt owed by an American today is now over $38,000. This amount does not include mortgages on homes.

I Timothy 3:3 says that a bishop *(pastor)* must not be covetous. When Moses chose men to oversee the children of Israel, he chose those "hating covetousness". (SEE EXODUS 18:21.).

God warns us of false prophets repeatedly. One way to recognize them is found in II Peter 2:3: "... **through covetousness** shall they with feigned *(insincere)* words make merchandise of you."

These false prophets and false teachers will twist the Scriptures to deceive their listeners. Their one motive will be wealth for themselves.

God told Israel, through His prophet Jeremiah, the cause of His wrath and pending judgment: "For from the least of them even unto the greatest of them every one is given to covetousness." JEREMIAH 6:13

God pleaded with His people to repent, as He described their sin: "Thine eyes and thine heart are not but for thy covetousness." JEREMIAH 22:17

He told Ezekiel, another one of His prophets, about the hearts of His chosen people: "... they come unto thee as the people cometh, and they sit before thee as my people, and they hear thy words, but they will not do them: for with their mouth they shew much love, but their heart goeth after their covetousness." EZEKIEL 33:31

A lawyer asked Jesus: "Master, which is the great commandment in the law?"

We should examine our hearts, as we read the answer Jesus gave: Jesus said unto him, Thou shalt love the Lord thy God with all thy heart, and with all thy soul, and with all thy mind. This is the first and great commandment." MATTHEW 22:36-38

Do we, as God's people, love Him with all our hearts, souls, and minds?

Or are our hearts filled with covetousness, which is based totally on love for self, rather than love for our Creator?

God often includes covetousness in His lists of sins that will bring His judgment upon mankind.

Romans 1:28-32 is one such list: "God gave them over to a reprobate mind, to do those things which are not convenient; being filled with all unrighteousness, fornication, wickedness, ***covetousness,*** maliciousness; full of envy, murder, debate, deceit, malignity; whisperers, backbiters, haters of God, despiteful, proud, boasters, inventors of evil things, disobedient to parents, without understanding, covenantbreakers, without natural affection, implacable, unmerciful: who knowing the judgment of God, that they which commit such things are worthy of death, not only do the same, but have pleasure in them that do them."

One of our problems is that covetousness is so prevalent in our American culture that we do not see it as SIN! God places a covetous person in the same category as a murderer or a hater of God! We just laughingly label it as "keeping up with the Joneses". The problem is that, while some try to keep up with the Joneses, the Joneses are trying to keep up with the Smiths, and the Smiths are trying to keep up with the Cunninghams. And no one ever quite arrives to a state of contentment.

God warns us of this: "For we dare not make ourselves of the number, or compare ourselves with some that commend themselves: but they measuring themselves by themselves, and comparing themselves among themselves, are not wise." II CORINTHIANS 10:12

When we compare ourselves to those who have *less* than we do, we become proud.

When we compare ourselves to those who have *more* than we do, it breeds discontent. We covet what they have, and begin life's fruitless cycle of becoming rich.

Proverbs 28:22 tells us: "He that hasteth to be rich hath an evil eye, and considereth not that poverty shall come upon him."

There is a promise of long life in the Word of God for all who meet its condition: "He that **hateth covetousness** shall prolong his days." PROVERBS 28:16

Peter looked upon his evil generation and thundered: "Save yourselves from this untoward *(crooked; perverse)* generation!" ACTS 2:40

How can we save ourselves from the sin of covetousness and greed, when we live in a society infested with it?

Should we go to the other extreme, give away all of our possessions, and live in a hut? Not necessarily. However, if that is what God asks us to do, we should obey willingly and immediately!

God has asked some to do this. One man ran and knelt before Jesus, asking, "Good Master, what shall I do that I may inherit eternal life?"

Jesus' reply was far different than most preachers would answer in our day. Most of them would have looked upon that young, eager, rich follower, and said, "Come be part of my ministry! Sell your goods, and bring me all of the proceeds!"

That was not the reply of Jesus. After the young man told Jesus that he had faithfully followed God's commandments, we read: "Jesus beholding him loved him, and said unto him, One thing thou lackest: go thy way, sell whatsoever thou hast, and **give to the poor**, and thou shalt have treasure in heaven: and come, take up the cross, and follow me." MARK 10:17 & 21

The young man's rejection of Jesus' call revealed three things:

1. He failed to keep God's first commandment. His heart, mind, and soul were not filled with love for God. He had reserved part of his heart, mind, and soul with love for his possessions.
2. He did not love his neighbor as himself. He was not willing to share his possessions with the poor.
3. The deadly sin of covetousness stood between him and Jesus.

We read his silent response to the Master's invitation: "He was sad at that saying, and went away grieved: for he had great possessions." MARK 10:21-22

Jesus did not call the young man back to tell him that he could just sell *part* of his possessions and still be His disciple. The young man's decision revealed that he loved his possessions more than he loved Jesus.

Jesus stood and watched him walk away. Then He turned to His disciples and said: "How hardly shall they that have riches enter into the kingdom of God!"

His disciples were astonished at His words. Then Jesus explained: "Children, how hard is it for them that **trust in riches** to enter into the kingdom of God!" MARK 10:23-24

God has asked many of His followers to forsake all material things for Him.

Yet, accompanied with His command, is this glorious promise: "...There is no man that hath left house, or brethren, or sisters, or father, or mother, or wife, or children, or lands, for my sake, and the gospel's, but he shall receive an hundredfold now in this time, houses, and brethren, and sisters, and mothers, and children, and lands, with persecutions; and in the world to come eternal life." MARK 10:29-30

Dedicated followers of Christ have traveled the world and have been received into homes by God's wonderful family.

One thing Christ desires of every single one of His followers. A follower of Jesus Christ must **be willing** to give up everything and keep nothing.

Jesus does not ask more of us than He gave Himself.

He gave up heaven, its streets of gold, its gates of pearl, His honor, His position - everything He had - to come to earth and begin His life on earth in a barn among animals.

Jesus said to one of His potential followers: "The foxes have holes, and the birds of the air have nests; but the Son of man hath not where to lay His head." MATTHEW 8:20

The devil offered Jesus all the kingdoms of this world and the glory that would come with them. The devil has nothing else to offer. He cannot offer us eternal life. He cannot offer us heaven. He was evicted from Heaven!

Jesus responded to Satan's offer with a rebuke: "Thou shalt worship the Lord thy God, and him only shalt thou serve." MATTHEW 4:10

Jesus borrowed a room to eat His last supper before His crucifixion.

Jesus rode a borrowed donkey into Jerusalem.

Jesus was buried in a borrowed tomb.

Jesus, our Example, lived a life of total sacrifice.

If Jesus is truly our Lord, He must also be Lord of our possessions. Everything He has given us should be for His use, not for our own. He is the One who has given us life, sight, a mind, strength, hands, health, and the ability to work.

God warned the children of Israel: "When thou hast eaten and art full, then thou shalt bless the Lord thy God for the good land which he hath given thee. Beware that thou forget not the Lord thy God ... lest when thou hast eaten and art full, and hast built goodly houses, and dwelt therein; and when thy herds and thy flocks multiply, and thy silver and thy gold is multiplied, and all that thou hast is multiplied; then thine heart be lifted up, and thou forget the Lord thy God ... and thou say in thine heart, My power and the might of mine hand hath gotten me this wealth. But thou shalt remember the Lord thy God: for it is he that giveth thee power to get wealth." DEUTERONOMY 8:10-14 & 17-18

If the Lord has given us a house, we should show hospitality in His name. Our tables should be set for the hungry sent by our Master. We should be willing to share our clothing with the needy. Our cars should be at the Lord's disposal, when He instructs us to provide transportation for others. When He speaks to us to give money to the poor, we should obey without hesitation.

God expects us to use the blessings He has given to us to bless others.

We should *always* be willing to walk away from every one of our possessions and remain content.

Jesus, and Jesus alone, is the Pearl of great price - our foremost Treasure. It is no loss to lose what we cannot keep to keep what we cannot lose! It is no loss to walk away from the things that are destined to be burned to walk toward what will last throughout eternity!

The rich young man walked away from Jesus, clutching his wealth in his heart. He lost every single one of his precious possessions. They are buried with his body under mountains of rubble. What a glorious life he would have had if he had followed Jesus! Instead of reading of his walking away from Christ, we would be reading of his running toward Him!

An old gravestone that marked the place of a dead man was engraved with these words:

WHAT I SPENT, I HAD.
WHAT I SAVED, I LOST.
WHAT I GAVE, I HAVE.

God demands that nothing come before Him in our affections. He wants our total love.

"If ye then be risen with Christ, seek those things which are above, where Christ sitteth on the right hand of God. Set your affection on things above, not on things on the earth. Lay not up for yourselves treasures upon earth, where moth and rust doth corrupt, and where thieves break through and steal: but lay up for yourselves treasures in heaven, where neither moth nor rust doth corrupt, and where thieves do not break through nor steal: for where your treasure is, there will your heart be also. No man can serve two masters: for either he will hate the one, and love the other; or else he will hold to the one, and despise the other. Ye cannot serve God and mammon." COLOSSIANS 3:1-2 AND MATTHEW 6:19-21 & 24

Mammon is *a passion for riches; a personification of the so-called goddess of wealth.* Countless idolaters fall at the feet of this goddess. Jesus knew that the rich young man would eventually leave Him, since his heart's desire was for the things of this life.

Jesus told us the following story of another man, whose total purpose in life was to lay up treasures for himself.

"... the ground of a certain rich man brought forth plentifully: and he thought within himself, saying, What shall I do, because I have no room where to bestow my fruits? And he said, This will I do: I will pull down my barns, and build greater; and there will I bestow all my fruits and my goods. And I will say to my soul, Soul, thou hast much goods laid up for many years; take thine ease, eat, drink, and be merry.

"But God said unto him, Thou fool, this night thy soul shall be required of thee: then whose shall those things be, which thou hast provided? So is he that layeth up treasure for himself, and is not rich toward God?" LUKE 12:16-21

If our motive for living is to gain material possessions, we will never have peace of mind. Such a life is doomed to failure. We may strive all of our lives to gain possessions, but we will **never** have quite enough. We will always want just one more car, one more insurance policy, one more deposit in our savings account, one more pair of shoes.

The wealthiest man on earth, King Solomon, finally came to this conclusion: "He that loveth silver shall not be satisfied with silver; nor he that loveth abundance with increase: this is also vanity. When goods increase, they are increased that eat them: and what good is there to the owners thereof, saving the beholding of them with their eyes?" ECCLESIASTES 5:10-11

As Solomon's appointment with death approached (as it will for each one of us) listen to his wail: "Yea, I hated all my labour which I had taken under the sun: because I should leave it unto the man that shall be after me. And who knoweth whether he shall be a wise man or a fool? yet shall he have rule over all my labour wherein I have laboured!" ECCLESIASTES 2:18-19

Now is the time to examine ourselves.

Are we happy if we have money?

Are we miserable if we don't?

Does money control our emotions?

Do we aimlessly browse through stores and find ourselves buying what we do not need?

Is there always a vague discontentment in our hearts?

Covetousness is the sin of America.

If we lived in Haiti, we would have to be spiritually alert so demonic voodoo practices did not become part of our lives.

If we lived in Russia, we would have to fight atheistic beliefs.

If we lived in India, we would have to avoid the worship of idols.

Those who live in America must fight valiantly against this sin of covetousness that pervades our country.

Be spiritually alert to the dangers of our society, rather than just drifting along and partaking of its sins.

Peace of mind and covetousness cannot walk together.

Contentment is **rest of mind; satisfaction; not inclined to desire something more or different than what one has**.

One of God's principles for financial peace of mind is that we leave no room in our hearts for covetousness. It is a deadly sin that we need to first recognize, then repent of, and finally to be delivered from.

"And having food and raiment let us be therewith content." I TIMOTHY 6:8

THE GOSPEL OF WEALTH

Jesus was rich, you say?
'Tis a twisted gospel indeed,
To fit our culture of this day,
that caters to man's greed.

It's the age old lie reborn,
spread by new breed of teacher,
Who views the poor with scorn,
while mocking the old-time preacher.

A new gospel, with a thirst
for a kingdom now and here;
That teaches men to seek Self first,
refusing God to fear.

They twist Christ's covenant of old;
His own blood, its decree.
They want silver and lots of gold!
Their wealth will set them free!

Choosing not to seek God's face,
they prefer to seek His hand.
Not enough, sins to erase!
God must serve, while they command.

For holiness, they don't thirst,
nor for godly doctrine sound.
They want their own desires first!
A new path they have found!

"Give us riches!   Give us more gold,
and mansions here so fine!
We will not walk the paths of old!
On this earth, we must shine!

God must give us our own way,
while we strut down here below.
For our desires, we will pray;
On Self, all goods bestow.

We choose to live in wealth,
and walk a path of great success.
In this life, naught but perfect health,
adorned with finest dress.

With the wealthy, we will dine;
and much gold we choose to seek.
Drinking only earth's best wine!
Being poor is for the meek!

Do you think we plan to lose?
I tell you; we will not be poor!
Our own selves, we will amuse!
We are destined to have more!

Let no man dare to take our coat;
nor slap our sun-kissed cheek.
We will sue him for his cloak!
Men will never find us weak!

Don't try to make us walk your mile,
or give us trial or test!
We're the heirs you must not rile!
We demand the very best!

We will get all that we claim,
and be all we wish to be.
Getting gold and much fame.
And even help you for a fee!

We choose to only serve a King
Who came to give us gold.
Not a Savior, who killed Death's sting,
to gain lambs for His fold.

Not enough is this new birth,
nor a heaven up above.
We want riches on this earth!
It's King Self we serve and love.

We are glad that God sent His Son,
who died on Calvary's hill.
But we want heaven and our fun,
and choose to do our will.

Yes, Jesus suffered on the cross;
His crown made up of thorn.
But we accept no trial or loss!
We're of royalty born!

Let this Jesus carry His cross!
We'll live our life of ease.
Let Him take all of the loss,
while we live just as we please.

Let God's own Son pay the price,
so we will have no sorrow.
We plan to have things nice,
with no tears in our tomorrow!

We are wise ones, men of fame;
the way of the cross, we mock.
We will never walk in shame.
Money is our founding rock."

Once again, prodigals spend all
for trinkets of this earth;
Refusing to heed our Lord's call,
They're blind to Christ's true worth.

Now if their fine words you have heard,
and wonder if they are right;
You must get back to God's own Word!
Be armed with sword and might!

Our Lord was loaned a humble womb;
placed in lowly stable;
Buried in a borrowed tomb.
Earthly riches?   A fable!

He walked among the needy poor,
the weak, the halt, the lame.
Touching wounded and the sore;
Never sought for earthly fame.

Rebuked the vain and proud;
Cared nothing for reputation.
To His Father's will, He bowed;
still cursed in every nation.

Satan offered to give Him all,
to catch in web and snare.
But He obeyed His Father's call,
trusting Him for His care.

He did not ride in pomp and style,
in gilded chariot of brass;
But walked the path of self-denial,
and rode on lowly ass.

His path led to Calvary's hill,
to the cross of terrible shame.
There, cruel men spilled His blood;
the purpose for which He came.

Few choose to follow our sweet Lord,
when asked to bear their cross.
But some follow in accord and,
for Him, count all things loss.

"Follow Me" still comes Christ's call,
"whatever may come your way."
His servants freely give Him all;
His will, not self, obey.

Marching through the centuries past,
no lust for wealth or fame;
Before His feet, their crowns will cast;
Praise only for His name.

Others live for Self alone;
to this world their souls sell;
Not enough is the blood He gave,
to free our souls from hell.

They will not follow the I AM;
new doctrines they devise.
And walk away from God's dear Lamb;
the Pearl of greatest prize.

Don't be moved away from Christ
by those who claim they are wise.
Don't trade Jesus for earth's gold,
nor heed men's alluring lies.

This earth will pass away.
Our promotion comes from above.
'til then, serve Christ, and obey!
Trust His never-failing love.

When God blesses, do not trust
the fleeting riches of earth.
For wealth here will surely rust.
Faith in Christ alone has worth.

Walk humbly, with no pride,
while on this earthly path you roam.
Be faithful, Christ's true Bride!
Heaven, not this earth, is your home!

Do not for wealth, salvation trade!
This life will soon be past.
Earth will burn and soon fade.
Priceless Pearl - Christ alone - will last.

Carolyn Wilde

STEP FOUR

FALSE BALANCES

Jesus turned to Peter one day with words that sent him on a strange errand: "Go thou to the sea, and cast an hook, and take up the fish that first cometh up; and when thou hast opened his mouth, thou shalt find a piece of money: that take, and give unto them for me and thee."

With this message, both a man and a fish were dispatched by their Creator for a divine appointment. Peter headed for the shore to catch a fish, and a fish headed for the spot where he had glimpsed a glittering coin and, picking it up in his mouth, swam toward Peter's hook to deliver it to him.

That was probably one of the strangest ways a preacher ever received an offering! Peter, a commercial fisherman who had caught thousands of fish, knew there was no earthly explanation for this miracle!

Why did the Son of God need money? Was He trying to finance His next missionary trip or evangelistic meeting? Did He need it to give to the poor?

The answer may surprise you. He needed money to pay taxes He did not even owe! It all began when they entered Capernaum.

Matthew tells us the story. "And when they were come to Capernaum, they that received tribute money came to Peter, and said, Doth not your master pay tribute? He saith, Yes. And when he was come into the house, Jesus prevented him, saying, What thinkest thou, Simon? of whom do the kings of the earth take custom or tribute? of their own children, or of strangers?

"Peter saith unto him, Of strangers. Jesus saith unto him, then are the children free. Notwithstanding, lest we should offend them …" MATTHEW 17:24-27

And you know the rest of the story. Peter was to catch the fish that was to deliver the coin and pay the undue tax!

The tribute was to be collected only from strangers passing through the land. Rather than arguing with and offending the greedy tax collectors, Jesus simply paid them the money. He did not demand His rights as a citizen and get entangled in a legal dispute. This would have caused offense to Him and to His message.

Instead, He just paid what He did not owe. By this one act, Jesus demonstrated another principle we must follow, if we want to be freed from money worries.

It is a sad reflection on today's society that many would rather do business with a sinner than with a professing Christian. Many "Christians" not only do not pay what they do **not** owe, they do not even pay what they **do** owe!

Their financial dealings are often unfair and dishonest, thus causing men to reject the message of the gospel of Jesus Christ.

Followers of Jesus should, above all men, diligently seek to follow our Lord's example by being just and fair in every financial dealing. We should be willing to do what is not legally required of us, in order to keep from offending men and thus bringing a reproach upon our Savior.

Yet, how many Christians are always fair and completely honest in their finances? God has much to say concerning our financial dealings with our fellow men.

Proverbs 11:1 says: "A false balance is abomination to the Lord: but a just weight is his delight!"

A false balance is a set of scales that is made to tip additional profit to its owner, weighing goods sold to the customer at a smaller weight.

Men call it good business.

God calls it an abomination.

Can we go to sleep at night, resting upon the promises of God, expecting His blessings, and having peace of mind, when we have treated our neighbor unfairly in order to gain more profit through deceit?

Have we forsaken and forgotten the ways and the words of our God in our greedy pursuit of the dollar?

Here are some of our Lord's commands. (Remember, as you read them, that they are not His **suggestions** - but His *commandments!*)

"Better is a little with righteousness than great revenues without right." PROVERBS 16:8

"Divers weights, and divers measures, both of them are alike abomination to the Lord." PROVERBS 20:10

"The getting of treasures by a lying tongue is a vanity tossed to and fro of them that seek death." PROVERBS 21:6

"A good name is rather to be chosen than great riches, and loving favour rather than silver and gold." PROVERBS 22:1

"Better is the poor that walketh in his uprightness, than he that is perverse in his ways, though he be rich." PROVERBS 28:6

"He that by usury and unjust gain increaseth his substance, he shall gather it for him that will pity the poor." PROVERBS 28:8

"Whoso is partner with a thief hateth his own soul." PROVERBS 29:24

"As the partridge sitteth on eggs, and hatcheth them not; so he that getteth riches, and not by right, shall leave them in the midst of his days, and at his end shall be a fool." JEREMIAH 17:11

Jeremiah sadly looked at God's children and gave this indictment: "From the prophet even unto the priest every one dealeth falsely." JEREMIAH 6:13

The prophet Micah cried out to his generation this warning from the very heart of God: "Are there yet the treasures of wickedness in the house of the wicked, and the scant measure that is abominable? Shall I count them pure with the wicked balances, and with the bag of deceitful weights? For the rich men thereof are full of violence, and the inhabitants thereof have spoken lies, and their tongue is deceitful in their mouth."

God's prophet then thundered our God's judgments: "Therefore also will I make thee sick in smiting thee, in making thee desolate because of thy sins. Thou shalt eat, but not be satisfied; and thy casting down shall be in the midst of thee; and thou shalt take hold, but shalt not deliver; and that which thou deliverest will I give up to the sword. Thou shalt sow, but thou shalt not reap; thou shalt tread the olives, but thou shalt not anoint thee with oil; and sweet wine, but shalt not drink wine ... ye shall bear the reproach of my people." MICAH 6:10-16

We cannot live with the peace and blessing of God and cheat our fellow man! God not only demands that we be just and fair in all of our dealings, He demands even more of His followers.

The following counsel of Jesus sounds strange in our day of self-centered greed, but stranger still would be a man who would be humble enough to obey His commandments!

"If any man will sue thee at the law, and take away thy coat, let him have thy cloak also!" MATTHEW 5:40

If Christians followed such a policy, the entire world's view of Christianity would be immediately revolutionized!

Instead, lawyers grow richer, representing professing Christians. God's people ignore God's commandments, as they sue and counter sue. Preachers and churches are told by their insurance agents that they must add malpractice to their policies, as they are being sued by so many church members. Preachers are even suing their denominations and other preachers. Churches are suing churches!

How far we have strayed from the Lord we profess to follow! We have become, not more like Him, but more like the world in our greedy pursuit of the dollar!

God explicitly commands Christians to **never** sue Christians. Could His words in I Corinthians 6:1-8 be any clearer?

"Dare any of you, having a matter against another, go to law before the unjust, and not before the saints? I speak to your shame. Is it so, that there is not a wise man among you? No, not one that shall be able to judge between his brethren? But brother goeth to law with brother, and that before the unbelievers. Now therefore there is utterly a fault among you, because ye go to law one with another. ***Why do ye not rather take wrong?*** Why do ye not rather suffer yourselves to be defrauded *(cheated; swindled)*?

"Nay, ye do wrong, and defraud *(illegally obtain money by deception)*, and that your brethren."

Many of today's television evangelists have become a laughing stock to the world, and no doubt a cause for weeping to our Lord. Too many of them have exchanged the Lord's beautiful gospel invitation for continuous begging for more money. It is little wonder that the world views Christians as being far more concerned with dollars than with souls.

Our nation has gone mad with its lust for the dollar. Men have even dared to label it *the almighty dollar*.

Jesus told us of the rich man in hell who belatedly realized that his eternal destiny lay, not in his wealth, but in his ALMIGHTY CREATOR.

Most men do not care if they have to trample on others to get more money.

One day soon our money system will collapse. Men who have staked their lives on their accumulation of money will literally weep and howl when they lose it all.

James prophesied of this time to come: "Go to now, ye rich men, weep and howl for your miseries that shall come upon you. Your riches are corrupted, and your garments are motheaten. Your gold and silver is cankered; and the rust of them shall be a witness against you, and shall eat your flesh as it were fire. Ye have heaped treasure together for the last days. Behold, the hire of the labourers who have reaped down your fields, which is of you kept back by fraud, crieth: and the cries of them which have reaped are entered into the ears of the Lord of sabaoth. Ye have lived in pleasure on the earth, and been wanton *(violent; cruel)*; ye have nourished your hearts, as in a day of slaughter. Ye have condemned and killed the just; and he doth not resist you." JAMES 5:1-6

Most employers and employees are so consumed with their own greed that they are willing to trample on others to benefit themselves. God's Word, if it was obeyed, would solve all of our labor problems, for God gives explicit advice to both employers and the employees.

"Servants, obey in all things your masters according to the flesh; not with eyeservice, as menpleasers; but in singleness of heart, fearing God: and whatsoever ye do, do it heartily, as to the Lord, and not unto men; knowing that of the Lord ye shall receive the reward of the inheritance: for ye serve the Lord Christ. But he that doeth wrong shall receive for the wrong which he hath done: and there is no respect of persons.

"Masters, give unto your servants that which is just and equal; knowing that ye also have a Master in heaven." COLOSSIANS 3:22-25 + 4:1

Sadly, it is unusual to find even a child of God with this spirit of selflessness and genuine love and concern for the welfare of others.

We live in a society in which an honest man is rare.

False advertising claims abound.

Citizens steal billions of dollars by cheating their government of taxes.

Man has sunk to a new low of dishonesty and craftiness. Rather than feel shame, most congratulate themselves for profiting at the expense of others.

Bookkeepers embezzle; salesmen lie; factory employees steal; shoppers lift; statesmen receive kickbacks; and computer operators devise new ways to transfer funds of others into their own accounts.

Men consistently falsify reports; sue and countersue; and claim undeserved money without even a twinge of guilt.

Far too many policemen and judges alike add to their wealth by receiving bribery payments and even by selling illegal drugs that they confiscate from criminals.

Scheming and conniving preachers have become a joke, as they deceive the ones they claim to be ministering to, in order to swell their offering plates.

Few men care whether their money is made honestly or dishonestly. Their only concern is that money is made!

God's Word describes the heart of man as desperately wicked and evil. However, God's true children have a new heart, a new life, and a love for mankind that causes them to deny themselves rather than to take financial advantage of others!

The prosperity teaching has not only crept - it has galloped - into the church that professes to follow Jesus. Scriptures are twisted and excuses are made, as professing Christians join the world in its deceitful methods for obtaining wealth.

Theft by employees is a major expense of every company. God says to His followers: "Let him that stole steal no more: but rather let him labour, working with his hands the thing which is good, that he may have to give to him that needeth." EPHESIANS 4:28

Roy was one of our first converts to the Lord Jesus Christ after we entered the ministry full time. When Roy received Jesus as his Savior, he also received Him as his Lord ... and that presented a problem for Roy. Roy knew that, as his Lord, Jesus would require that he make things right with his employer. After much prayer, Roy sat in his boss's office, confessing his sins.

"I want to return the tools and the other things I have stolen from this factory during the years I worked here."

His boss was shocked - not to learn that Roy had stolen from the factory - but that he wanted to make things right! The factory was full of employees who stole on a regular basis and thought nothing of it!

It took a while to work out the details of inventory and bookkeeping adjustments, but Roy was able to make full restitution. He asked if the amount he owed could be deducted from his future paychecks until all that he felt he owed was repaid. Roy became a vibrant testimony to our Lord's transforming power!

If all who claim to be born again Christians would follow Jesus and obey His commandments, there would be a revival! Instead, conviction of sins is seldom the result of today's watered-down gospel of prosperity. As a result, restitution is seldom practiced voluntarily today. Few preachers are preaching the same message that Jesus preached, as they are only too willing to deceive and mislead their congregations who no longer want the truth. It is sad that many of today's prophets are concerned only with their profits.

Our country's leaders have plunged our nation so deeply in debt that we are on the verge of national bankruptcy. It was recently stated however, that if all those who cheat on their income taxes would pay the government what they rightfully owe for taxes, our nation would be debt free!

Man cheats God.

Man cheats his government.

Man cheats man.

Few are concerned about what God calls sin.

Men who wished to ensnare Jesus asked Him whether or not it was lawful for Rome to demand taxes of them.

"Is it lawful to give tribute to Caesar, or not?" they asked.

Jesus asked them for a penny, and holding it before them, answered with a question of His own: "Whose is the image and superscription?"

Their answer was: "Caesar's."

"And Jesus answering said unto them, render to Caesar the things that are Caesar's, and to God the things that are God's." (SEE MARK 12:13-17.)

Jesus clearly taught that men are to pay the taxes that their government requires of them. Where would our nation be if no one paid their rightful taxes? We would have no highways, bridges, fire or police protection, prisons, courtrooms, or defense against invading armies.

"Render to Caesar the things that are Caesar's," our Lord commanded. Caesar was an ungodly ruler of an ungodly nation. Yet, his sins and the sin of the Roman government did not excuse the nation's citizens from paying their taxes.

Is it possible to have financial peace of mind and defraud our neighbor, our employer, and our government?

Can we sleep peacefully at night, knowing that we have been unfair in our dealings with others during the day?

Dare we lie, steal, and cheat, while calling ourselves Christians ... followers of Jesus Christ?

Dare we pray for God to bless us when we are hurting others?

Ananias and his wife, Sapphira, were struck dead in the middle of a revival meeting because they lied to the Holy Ghost about money!   (SEE ACTS 5:1-11.)

Should we lightly vow to pay a bill, and then make no effort to keep our promise?

Should we go to every possible length to cheat and evade payment of our taxes, even as we heartily sing, "God Bless America" and wave a flag?

Should a Christian employer pay the lowest wage possible?

Should an employee, who calls himself a Christian, shirk his duties, lie on his expense account, call in sick when he wants a day off, and then strike for higher wages than his employer can reasonably pay?

Should a salesman include lies in his sales pitch?

Should we sell our neighbor a car, claiming it runs well, when we know it is in need of expensive repairs?   Should we make claims that are untrue, in order to profit from a sale?

As long as we refuse to treat others as we wish to be treated, we will have no financial peace of mind.

There will be no blessing from God upon our lives.

God hates the false balance that robs a customer of his rightful goods. He despises our modern ways of dishonesty that rob and cheat our fellow men.

"But everybody is doing it," is no excuse.

Everybody is *not* doing it. There are still a few honest people in this corrupt world.

Are you one of them?

We need to be willing to obey God's principle of going the second mile with people.

We need to be willing to follow our Master's example, even if it means paying what we do not rightfully owe.

We need to treat everyone fairly, even when it means we take a loss. God will make up for our losses with His continual blessings!

Unless we are willing to follow this principle with all men, we will never have financial peace of mind. God will not bless those who deal with false balances!

STEP FIVE

A GIVING SPIRIT

A little fellow in the slum section of Chicago was invited to attend a mission Sunday School. He went, and he received Jesus as his Savior and became a faithful little Christian.

One day, someone said to him, "If God loves you so much, why doesn't He take better care of you? Why doesn't He tell someone to bring you shoes and a warm coat and better food?"

This little fellow thought for a moment. Then, with tears in his eyes, he said: "I guess He does tell somebody. But somebody forgets."

Somebody forgets.

Or somebody simply does not care.

Or possibly somebody rebels.

Or perhaps somebody judges and condemns the boy or his parents and refuses to help him.

One thing is sure: **somebody does not have a giving spirit**.

God says: "... whoso hath this world's good, and seeth his brother have need, and shutteth up his bowels of compassion from him, how dwelleth the love of God in him? My little children, let us not love in word, neither in tongue; but in deed and in truth."   I JOHN 3:17-18

Christianity itself is based on giving.

God gave His Son.

Jesus gave His blood.

The Holy Ghost gave His power, His fruit, and His gifts.

Jesus' disciples gave up all they had to follow Christ.

The church, born at Pentecost, gave up their possessions, laying them at the apostles' feet, so the gospel could be preached.

The apostles gave the ultimate sacrifice and became martyrs, rather than denying their Lord and His message. Yet, no man could out give Jesus.

Jesus gives us forgiveness, love, daily blessings, eternal life, an eternal home, and literally divides His inheritance with us!

When we enter this world, it begins to teach us the way of man ... **GET**!

When we are born again into God's family, He begins to change our nature and teach us His way ... **GIVE**!

Until we become people with a giving spirit, rather than a *getting* spirit, we will *never* have financial peace of mind.

Peace of mind comes only from Jesus, the Prince of Peace.

A giving spirit is the very foundation of Christianity. Jesus expects us to willingly give ourselves, our strength, our talents, our time, and our possessions when He calls for them!

The Bible, from Genesis to Revelation, teaches giving. Listen, as God counsels us: "If there be among you a poor man of one of thy brethren within any of thy gates in thy land which the Lord thy God giveth thee, thou shalt not harden thine heart, nor shut thine hand from thy poor brother: But thou shalt open thine hand wide unto him, and shalt surely lend him sufficient for his need, in that which he wanteth." DEUTERONOMY 15:7-8

"The liberal soul shall be made fat: and he that watereth shall be watered also himself." PROVERBS 11:25

Liberal means *possessing or manifesting a free and generous heart.*

"... he that hath mercy on the poor, happy is he." PROVERBS 14:21

"... he that oppresseth the poor reproacheth his Maker: but he that honoureth him hath mercy on the poor."

"He that hath pity upon the poor lendeth unto the Lord; and that which he hath given will he pay him again." PROVERBS 19:17

"Whoso stoppeth his ears at the cry of the poor, he also shall cry himself, but shall not be heard." PROVERBS 21:13

"He that hath a bountiful *(generous)* eye shall be blessed; for he giveth of his bread to the poor."   PROVERBS 22:9

"He that giveth unto the poor shall not lack: but he that hideth his eyes shall have many a curse."   PROVERBS 28:27

Paul instructed the young preacher, Timothy: "Charge them that are rich in this world, that they be not high-minded, nor trust in uncertain riches, but in the living God, who giveth us richly all things to enjoy; that they do good, that they be rich in good works, ready to distribute, willing to communicate *(share with others)*."   I TIMOTHY 6:17-18

God describes the characteristics of a virtuous woman. One of them is a giving spirit.

"She stretcheth out her hand to the poor; yea, she reacheth forth her hands to the needy."   PROVERBS 31:20

God tells us that it is not enough to just offer the peace of God to one who is hungry or naked. Listen closely to His full instructions: "If a brother or sister be naked, and destitute of daily food, and one of you say unto them, Depart in peace, be ye warmed and filled; notwithstanding ye give them not those things which are needful to the body; what doth it profit?"   JAMES 2:15-16

Jesus said: "He that hath two coats, let him impart to him that hath none; and he that hath meat, let him do likewise."   LUKE 3:11

Jesus also said, "Give, and it shall be given unto you; good measure, pressed down, and shaken together, and running over, shall men give into your bosom. For with the same measure that ye mete withal it shall be measured to you again." Luke 6:38

You determine the measure you will use when you give!

If you give a teaspoonful, you will be given a teaspoonful back from God, pressed down, shaken together and running over!

If you use a cup for your measure, God will return to you a cup full of blessings, heaped up and overflowing!

If you fill a bushel and give it to others, God will use your bushel for His measure and fill it up with overflowing blessings!

You have probably heard the expression: "We can't out give God!" It is true. The reason it is impossible to out give God is because He takes the measure we have used to give blessings to others. Then He fills it up with blessings for us! He heaps blessings up in our measure until they are literally running over the sides!

God is a giving God!

God wants His children to represent their Father well, by being a giving people! God has blessed us, so we can share His blessing of giving to others.

The apostle Paul wrote: "Ye ought to support the weak, and to remember the words of the Lord Jesus, how he said, It is more blessed to give than to receive." Acts 20:35

It pleases God to bless His people. He wants you to share the pleasure of giving with Him.

Jesus said, "If ye know these things, happy are ye if ye do them!" John 13:17

We could invert this verse and say: "If ye know these things, miserable are ye if ye don't do them!"

God is continually looking for people to bless. We read in II Chronicles 16:9: "For the eyes of the Lord run to and fro throughout the whole earth, to shew himself strong in the behalf of them whose heart is perfect toward him."

If we will join God in His business of blessing people, we will soon discover that the real blessing is in giving, rather than in receiving!

God's plan is to use us to give to people He wants to bless!

Did you notice that when Jesus said: "Give, and it shall be given unto you; good measure, pressed down, and shaken together, and running over", He went on to say that *men* would give into our bosom?

God often works through men to distribute His blessings. He blesses people through His children who have the same generous spirit that He has!

We need to be continually aware that God answers the prayers of the poor *through us!*

How many prayers go unanswered because we are not listening to our Lord's instructions, as He tells us to deliver food to the hungry; give clothing to the naked; or give money to the needy? We cannot even comprehend how many blessings we miss, when we do not have a giving spirit!

There are several reasons why some do not have a giving spirit.

Some may be so self-centered and self-absorbed that they simply do not think of the needs of others.

Some are so covetous that their thoughts are only about themselves. They neither consider nor care that their neighbors are hungry.

Some are too judgmental to give and they show no mercy for the poor. Instead, they try, judge, pronounce guilty, condemn to poverty, and proudly refuse to help them.

Thank God for His mercy on us! Who among us has not made mistakes?

God, who is perfect, has such a beautiful spirit of giving that He blesses all mankind!

Matthew 5:45 tells us: "He maketh His sun to rise on the evil and on the good, and sendeth rain on the just and on the unjust!"

Not one of us deserves God's blessings!

If no one extended mercy to the poor, there would be no missions for the homeless; no hospitals or doctors who would treat those who could not afford treatment; and no food distributed to the hungry. People in every village, town, and city of our nation would be in our streets begging, starving, freezing, and dying of their diseases.

The elderly who are poor would be cast in our streets to die.

Our streets would overflow with the mentally and physically handicapped.

It is true that some do starve or freeze, but these are few, compared to the vast numbers of poor who are cared for and fed by the merciful.

No one but our Master has lived a perfect life.

If we hold a ***judgmental*** spirit toward the poor, we cannot at the same time have a ***giving spirit*** of mercy toward them.

Jesus told us that in order to obtain mercy from God, we must have mercy on others! "Blessed are the merciful: for they shall obtain mercy." MATTHEW 5:7

One of the reasons we do not give to the poor is because we have already given our tithes to God. Many feel this is sufficient.

But is it? Or is it only the foundation of a giving spirit?

Dare we give God less than a tenth of our income?

He has freely given everything to us.

"He that spared not his own Son, but delivered him up for us all, how shall he not with him also freely give us all things?" ROMANS 8:32

We have nothing without God!

We do not even have our existence without God!

"Every good gift and every perfect gift is from above, and cometh down from the Father of lights, with whom is no variableness, neither shadow of turning." JAMES 1:17

God created us! He breathed His very breath into us, giving us life!

He gave us a body, so we could work.

He gave us a mind, so we could think and reason.

He formed a beautiful earth for our home.

He gave us air to breathe.

He gave us water to drink.

He is the Giver of seeds, so we can plant and reap a harvest of fruits, grains, and vegetables.

He is the One who placed a sun above us to warm us, give us light, and nourish our seeds so they would grow.

He is the One who sends rain upon our crops. Without the gift of rain, we could toil, but would never reap a harvest.

God created animals, birds, and fish for our pleasure and our food.

God planted the trees that we use to build houses and furnishings.

God created us with a built-in reproductive system, so we can bear children and delight in them.

It is God who gives us our daily strength, so we can continue to labor.

It is God who has appointed His angels to minister to us.

God has given us the physical strength and mental ability to perform work.

Man responded to God's wonderful provisions with rebellion against His commandments.

God sent compassionate leaders and prophets to woo men back to Him; to warn them of the consequences of sin; to remind them of His judgments; and to plead with them to return to their merciful Creator.

Man responded by stoning His prophets.

God, who is rich in love and grace, responded to man's sins with the Gift of His precious Son.

Jesus went about, doing good.

Man responded by beating Him, mocking Him, nailing Him to a cross, and sealing His tomb, lest He rise from the dead and continue His good works.

God was silent, as Jesus writhed in agony, inflicted by the cruelty of men.

Jesus could have called angels to rescue Him from the cross and destroy all of mankind.

Instead, He suffered and died ... for us.

God's gift of the blood of His only begotten Son is for our eternal salvation.

His plan of redemption is to bring us to His home in Heaven, where He has prepared a place for us that is beyond our imagination.

I Corinthians 2:9 tells us that "eye hath not seen, nor ear heard, neither have entered into the heart of man, the things which God hath prepared for them that love him."

Do we dare give our wonderful Creator nothing in return?

Do we dare serve ourselves, rather than serving Him?

Do we dare to even question whether we should give Him ten percent of our income?

Our tithe is not given to enrich God!

God uses our tithe to enrich our spiritual lives!

He uses it to provide for His servants, as they minister among us. He uses it to send missionaries with the wonderful message of salvation throughout the world.

He uses it to house orphans and feed the hungry.

He uses it to provide places for His people to assemble and strengthen one another.

He uses it to spread His Word of Truth throughout this world of lies, so men, women, and children will read the Bible, and come to Him for salvation and deliverance.

Our giving is God's plan to bless us and to carry on His work.

Malachi 3:10 instructs us to: 'Bring ye all the tithes into the storehouse, that there may be meat in mine house, and prove me now herewith, saith the Lord of hosts, if I will not open you the windows of heaven, and pour you out a blessing, that there shall not be room enough to receive it."

We give Him our tithe!

He then uses our gift to pour blessings from Heaven down upon us!

THIS IS OUR GOD!

Perhaps one of the most beautiful examples of tithing is found in Richard Wurmbrand's book, *Tortured for Christ*. Richard suffered for many years in Communist prisons because of his unwavering faith in Christ. His suffering included torture and near starvation. Yet, **Richard tithed**. He was given only one slice of bread a week. Every tenth week, he gave his bread to a prisoner, in Jesus' name.

Each day, he was given a bowl of dirty soup. Every tenth day, Richard found a brother who was physically weaker than himself, and gave him his soup, in Jesus' name.

Paying our tithes is the very foundation of a giving heart. We should count it joy to give to our giving God!

God says: "Honour the Lord with thy substance, and with the firstfruits of all thine increase: so shall thy barns be filled with plenty, and thy presses shall burst out with new wine!" PROVERBS 3:9-10

However, paying our tithes is only the foundation upon which we must build.

God's people seem to think that their giving begins and ends with their tithe. Under the Old Covenant, tithing was demanded. A tithe simply means a ***tenth***. God's people were commanded to give one tenth of everything they had - not only money, but their harvests, their herds, their flocks - everything.

Some of God's people of our generation argue that tithing is a commandment given only to the Israelites, and it does not need to be obeyed today. It is true that Jesus did not teach His followers to tithe. He instead told them to give everything! The closest He came to teaching tithing was in one of His rebukes to the scribes and Pharisees. "Woe unto you, scribes and Pharisees, hypocrites! for ye pay tithe of mint and anise and cummin, and have omitted the weightier matters of the law, judgment, mercy, and faith: ***these ought ye to have done***, and not to leave the other undone." MATTHEW 23:23

Jesus told them that they did right in paying tithes on even their spices. Then He went on to say that, even though they had done their duty by paying their tithes, they left the most important things out of their lives. They left out judgment, mercy, and faith!

It takes faith to have mercy! Often, when God tells us to have mercy on the poor and to give away the last penny we have, we disobey because we worry about our own needs. We do not obey Him, because we lack faith that God will provide for us!

Jesus sat by the offering basket and watched people cast in their money. Mark tells us about it. "And Jesus sat over against the treasury, and beheld how the people cast money into the treasury: and many that were rich cast in much. And there came a certain poor widow, and she threw in two mites, which make a farthing. And he called unto him his disciples, and saith unto them, Verily I say unto you, that this poor widow hath cast more in, than all they which have cast into the treasury: for all they did cast in of their abundance; but she of her want did cast in *all that she had, even all her living*." MARK 12:41-44

Jesus did not commend the rich who paid their tithes. **He commended the widow with the giving spirit**! She gave all her living! She had faith that God would then take care of her. She literally put her life into God's hands.

Do you think that our God, who cares for the sparrow, watched that widow give everything she had to Him, and then allowed her to starve to death? I believe He provided abundantly and miraculously for her needs!

Yet, the Pharisees had no such faith in a God that could feed and clothe them. Neither did they have mercy upon the poor. All they could say at the end of their lives was that they had paid their tithes.

Jesus told us about a Pharisee who stood in the temple praying. He boasted to God: "I give tithes of all that I possess!" LUKE 18:12

Jesus said that the Pharisee did not leave justified. Jesus demands more of His followers than just paying tithes. He demands complete control of all of our possessions!

He did not instruct the rich young ruler who desired to follow Him to pay his tithes. Instead, He said: "Sell ALL that thou hast, and distribute unto the poor, and thou shalt have treasure in heaven: and come, follow me!" LUKE 18:22

Our tithes, or tenth, is the very least we can give God. We begin with our tithe. Then, if He tells us to give to the poor or to His work, we must be willing to give more than our tenth. We cannot expect His blessings if we withhold anything that He asks of us! All that we have - including our lives - belongs to Him! If He tells us to give all, as the early church did, then we are to give one-hundred per cent, not ten per cent!

R. G. LeTournou, who designed and built heavy earth moving equipment, was not satisfied after giving God his tithe. He began by giving God his tenth. Then he increased his giving. Before his death, he was keeping ten per cent of his income and giving God ninety percent. When he died, he was still a multi-millionaire!

J. L. Kraft, head of *Kraft Cheese*, said: "The only investments I ever made which have paid constantly increasing dividends is the money I have given to the Lord." For many years, Mr. Kraft gave 25 percent of his income to Christian causes.

William Colgate started one of the oldest companies in America. The *Colgate-Palmolive Company* is nearly two-hundred years old. William had to leave his home at the age of sixteen. His father was too poor to keep him, so he sent him out into the world to make his own way. All William owned was tied in a bundle that he carried in his hand. When he found a job in New York, the first thing he did with the first dollar he earned was to give his tithe to the Lord. As the Lord began to bless him, he soon began giving twenty percent of his income to the Lord. He raised it to thirty percent - then to forty percent - then to fifty percent. In the later years of his life, William Colgate was giving one-hundred percent of his annual income to the Lord. How many of us miss God's blessings because we are unwilling to give Him more than His tenth? He often asks more of His people!

It was not enough for the widow woman who was asked by Elijah for a little meal to just give him ten percent of what she had. Elijah wanted a full share in her last meal. He not only wanted his food first, he wanted thirty-three per cent of her food! What a blessing she would have missed if she had stopped with her tithe! She had a giving spirit, and God provided food for her in the midst of the famine. She is a beautiful example of God's promises in Psalm 33:18-19: "Behold, the eye of the Lord is upon them that fear him, upon them that hope in his mercy; to deliver their soul from death, and to keep them alive in famine."

Should we give God His tenth? How can we think of doing less? If there is a question whether or not God would expect us to pay a tithe on a certain income or gift, pay it! You can't out give God! Give to God immediately and joyfully! He has blessed you with every increase!

The most important question is: do *you* have a giving spirit?

Can God depend on *you* to have mercy on the poor?

Can He use *you* to answer men's prayers?

Can He use *you* to provide a channel that He can work through to bless others?

We all need to have a giving spirit, both toward God and toward men. We are reminded that God Himself said that when we give to the poor, we are lending Him money! Dare we believe that God would not pay His debt?

Countless martyrs down through the ages gave God their very lives. God returned their gift with eternal life!

In order to have financial peace of mind, we must be obedient to the voice of God. We need to be always ready to give whatever He asks of us ... even if He asks us for one-hundred percent!

We need to pray: "Oh, God! Change my **getting** spirit into a **giving** spirit!"

We may think that we have too little to give. No gift is too small.

The widow of the Old Testament gave a meal.

The widow of the New Testament gave her mite.

A little lad gave his lunch.

Richard Wurmbrand gave his bowl of dirty soup and his slice of moldy bread.

And Hattie, a poor little girl who lived in Philadelphia, Pennsylvania over one-hundred years ago, gave an incredible gift. Hattie gave her Lord fifty-seven cents.

Hattie not only had no nice clothes or any toys, she often went to bed hungry. Yet, Hattie yearned for only one thing. She wanted to go to Sunday School in the little church near her home. Every Sunday morning, Hattie walked to the little church building to watch the children go to Sunday School. She listened to their happy singing. She tried so hard to hear the stories their teachers were telling. She liked hot summer days best. Then the teachers opened the windows and she could hear all the wonderful stories about Jesus. She looked at the children's smiling faces when they came out of Sunday School, and dreamed of being invited inside, even if it was just once.

Pastor Russell Conwell often noticed the little girl standing outside, watching and listening. He went over to Hattie one day, and said, "Little Girl, one day maybe we will have a building big enough so you can come in. Right now, our Sunday School building is very crowded with children. We don't have any room for you."

Hattie sadly went home, hungry, and shivering in the cold. Yet, her physical hunger paled when compared to the hunger in her soul. She longed to hear more stories about Jesus. She thought of other poor children, and wished that there was room for all of them in the little **Grace Baptist Church** on the corner. How the Bible stories would warm their hearts!

But what could Hattie do? She was just one little girl who didn't have any money or any way to help the church make room for poor children. Then Hattie had an idea. There *was* something she could do, and she found a treasure that would help her do it! She found an old empty purse! Now all she had to do was to get to work! Hattie carried sacks for people. She swept porches. Every penny she earned went into her little ragged purse. Hattie counted her pennies every day.

Then one frigid morning, Hattie Mae awoke coughing, shivering, hot with fever, and hardly able to walk.

Yet, even while Hattie's malnourished body was failing, her dream did not fade. She knew she was dying, and she had one request for her mother: "Mama, please tell Pastor Conwell from the church down the street to have my funeral. He was nice to me."

Her parents granted her request, and contacted the pastor when Hattie died. He arrived at their home, looked at the still form on the bed, and gasped. "Why this is the little girl who stood in the cold outside the church listening to the children sing. I wanted to invite her inside, but we just didn't have enough room."

Hattie's mother realized that the pastor didn't even know Hattie's name. She told him: "My daughter's name is Hattie Mae Wiatt. She told me you were nice to her. She knew that she was dying, and she asked me to send for you to conduct her funeral."

Her voice sharpened with her next words: "Will there be room for Hattie's cold, lifeless body in your church?"

The pastor could only say, "Yes. I will make room for Hattie Mae." He then turned and left the cold house.

Hattie's father stopped him. "Wait, Reverend. Our Hattie left something for you."

The pastor paused. "What do you mean? What could Hattie leave for me?"

Hattie's mother handed Pastor Conwell a ragged purse. "Hattie told me to give this to you. There is a note to you inside."

The pastor counted out 57 pennies, then unfolded the note from the little girl who had labored with a hungry stomach, a cold body, and a giving heart.

"I am giving all my money to you. Please build a church big enough so all the children who want to come to your Sunday School will have room."

Fifty-seven cents.

It seems so small today, but in 1886 it was a lot of money for a poor little girl to have. She could have bought a warm coat, mittens, a bonnet, and even a beautiful doll with the money she had earned. Yet, it was hardly enough to build a new church! Or was it? What could Hattie's little gift of 57 cents do?

Pastor Conwell told Hattie's story to his little congregation, and they formed the **Wiatt Mite Society**. Members told the story of Hattie Mae and her gift of 57 cents to everyone who would listen. A man heard the story and came to the church with a strange request. "I want to buy little Hattie's pennies. I want to be reminded of her great sacrifice. I will pay $250 for Hattie's little red purse with its 57 pennies."

That was a lot of money! It was enough at that time to buy a house and turn it into a Sunday School! And that's what the church did. Children began to come to the new Sunday School and learn about Jesus.

Hattie's fifty-seven pennies were returned to the church and displayed. People began coming to church just to look at those pennies. Moved, they dropped their pennies and their dollars into the offering box beside her pennies. The box filled up again and again. The church purchased land for more buildings. As Hattie's gift grew, the church grew.

If you go to Philadelphia, be sure to visit the church that Hattie's pennies built. For the little church that had no room for Hattie now seats 3,300 people.

The little church that had no room for Hattie now has a university where thousands of young people are educated.

The little church that had no room for Hattie now has the *Good Samaritan Hospital* that cares for sick children. A picture hangs on a wall in the hospital. The picture shows Hattie in a beautiful dress, even though she never had one. But the face is still Hattie's sweet little face. It is the beautiful face of the little girl whose 57 cents was turned into a great church, a great university, and a great children's hospital.

No gift that is given to the Lord with a heart full of love is small in His eyes. Jesus can still multiply the gifts we offer to Him, whether it be a lad's small lunch or a ragged purse that contains 57 hard-earned pennies.

When our gifts are placed in our Lord's nail-pierced hand, He will minister physical and spiritual food to vast numbers of people. Our wonderful Lord will bless and multiply every sacrifice that is given from a heart full of love for Him and for others. Not one offering is too small for Him to use.

After all, God used one of Adam's rib to make the first woman!

WE CAN NEVER OUTGIVE OUR LORD

She poured out sweet perfume,
In the midst of men's sneers.
She knelt down before Him,
Bathed His feet with her tears.

Man's scorns seemed as nothing,
To her heart filled with love.
She can't outgive Jesus,
Her sweet Lord from above.

Jesus poured out His blood.
He suffered in shame.
All creation stood by,
As men mocked His dear name.

He prevented angels,
From defending with sword.
Not one will be able
To outgive the Lord.

We can give Him our life,
Count our own as a loss.
We can kneel before Him,
At that old rugged cross.

We can follow His steps,
Give our head to man's sword.
But no man can ever
Outgive Jesus, our Lord.

Carolyn Wilde

STEP SIX

GOD FIRST

One of the scribes approached Jesus as He was teaching and asked Him: "Which is the first commandment of all?

"And Jesus answered him, The first of all the commandments is, Hear, O Israel; The Lord our God is one Lord: and thou shalt love the Lord thy God with all thy heart, and with all thy soul, and with all thy mind, and with all thy strength: this is the first commandment." MARK 12:28-30

First simply means **preceding all others**.

Unless we are obedient to this first and greatest of all commandments, we will never have financial peace of mind, for God's blessing will not be upon our lives.

Under the Old Covenant, the Israelites were commanded to give God the first of their harvests, the first males of their flocks and herds, and even their firstborn sons. "Sanctify unto me all the firstborn," God said, and "Whatsoever openeth the womb among the children of Israel, both of man and of beast: it is mine." EXODUS 13:2

Jesus commands His followers to "Seek ye **first** the kingdom of God, and his righteousness." MATTHEW 6:33

If the disciples of Jesus had not been willing to obey His commandment to put Him first, we would not even know the gospel message!

Peter and Andrew were men who put God first. They were fishermen, working to support their families, when Jesus walked along the shore.

"And Jesus, walking by the sea of Galilee, saw two brethren, Simon called Peter, and Andrew his brother, casting a net into the sea: for they were fishers. And he saith unto them, Follow me, and I will make you fishers of men. And they straightway left their nets, and followed him." MATTHEW 4:18-20

Peter and Andrew walked away from their nets - their very living - and put Jesus first in their lives.

James and John were two more brothers who put Jesus first - before all else.

"And going on from thence, he saw other two brethren, James the son of Zebedee, and John his brother, in a ship with Zebedee their father, mending their nets; and he called them. And they immediately left the ship and their father, and followed him." MATTHEW 4:21-22

James and John walked away from their broken nets - their unfinished work - and their father, to follow their new Master.

Matthew was collecting taxes when Jesus passed by.

"And as Jesus passed forth from thence, he saw a man, named Matthew, sitting at the receipt of custom: and he saith unto him, Follow me. And he arose, and followed him."

Jesus spoke just two words to Matthew, but they were enough to cause Matthew to immediately leave his job, income, and living. He did not give his employer a two weeks' notice. He did not seek a replacement for his job. He simply walked away from everything to put Jesus Christ first from that day forward. Nearly two-thousand years later, we are still quoting from the book Matthew wrote to tell us about his walk with Jesus.

Later, Paul heard the voice of God. The first words Paul spoke to Jesus were: "Lord, what wilt thou have me to do?" ACTS 9:6

Those eight words changed the rest of Paul's life. Paul made a whole-hearted commitment to put Jesus before all else and before all others.

Listen to Paul, as he tells us about that life-changing decision: "But what things were gain to me, those I counted loss for Christ. Yea doubtless, and I count all things but loss for the excellency of the knowledge of Christ Jesus my Lord: for whom I have suffered the loss of all things, and do count them but dung, that I may win Christ." PHILIPPIANS 3:7-8

Marching through the pages of both the Old and New Testaments, we meet a great army of people who obeyed

God's one commandment to put Him **first** in all areas of their lives.

Abraham left his people, his religion, and his country to follow the call of God.

Moses was a man who could have had all the riches and power of Egypt, but he put God first. Moses "refused to be called the son of Pharaoh's daughter, choosing rather to suffer affliction with the people of God, than to enjoy the pleasures of sin for a season; esteeming the reproach of Christ greater riches than the treasures in Egypt." HEBREWS 11:24-26

Elisha was plowing in the field with twelve yokes of oxen when Elijah passed by and threw his mantle over him. Elisha understood that God was calling him to take Elijah's place as His prophet.

Elisha left the oxen, the field, his farm, and literally ran after Elijah. He had only one request: "Let me, I pray thee, kiss my father and my mother, and then I will follow thee!" Can you see him running into the house, kissing his parents, and hurrying to catch Elijah? The kisses marked the ending of his old life. Elisha's decision to obey God marked the beginning of his new life. Elisha put God first from that day forward. (SEE I KINGS 19:19-21.)

Jesus Himself wept in great agony in the Garden of Gethsemane, as He saw the cross before Him. He put His Father's will *first* in His life, as He prayed: "Thy will be done." If He had not put His Father's will before His own, there would be no cross, no gospel, no salvation, no Savior, no hope, no eternal life, and no invitation to heaven.

If Christ's disciples had not put God's will *first* in their lives, the gospel message would have faded away in the first century.

If there were not men and women today who seek God *first*, the light of the gospel would not shine in our generation. Darkness would prevail.

The Bible also tells us about many who rejected God's call to give Him first place in their lives.

Adam and Eve gave up the fellowship and blessing of God for a bite of forbidden fruit. Their decision bought them sorrow and death. They buried their younger son and watched as their other son, a murderer, walked away from them. All humanity suffers today because they put their appetites first, rather than putting God first.

Esau followed their example. He sold his birthright to his younger brother for a bowl of soup. He is referred to in the New Testament as a "profane person, who for one morsel of meat sold his birthright". (SEE HEBREWS 12:16.) Food came before God in Esau's life.

Possessions held first place in King Saul's life. He was commanded by Samuel to smite Amalek and to "utterly destroy all that they have, and spare them not; but slay both man and woman, infant and suckling, ox and sheep, camel and ass." Saul planned to obey, but greed for the bounty of war changed his mind. The Bible tells us that Saul kept the best of the sheep, oxen, fatlings, lambs, and all that was good, and refused to destroy them. Saul put animals before God. God said: "It repenteth me that I have set up Saul to be king." (SEE I SAMUEL, CHAPTER 15.)

Naaman was healed of leprosy when he followed Elisha's counsel to dip seven times in the Jordan River. Naaman was so thankful for his healing that he offered Elisha ten talents of silver, six thousand pieces of gold, and ten changes of raiment. Elisha refused payment for the miracle only God could give. However, Elisha's servant, Gehazi, bitterly watched Naaman leave, with his chariot full of riches. The spirit of greed filled him until he could stand still no longer.

He ran to overtake Naaman's chariot. "My master hath sent me," he lied, "saying, Behold, even now there be come to me from mount Ephraim two young men of the sons of the prophets: give them, I pray thee, a talent of silver, and two changes of garments."

Later, as Gehazi stood before Elisha, Elisha asked him where he had been. He lied again: "No where."

Elisha knew what he had done. "Is it a time to receive money, and to receive garments?" he thundered. "The leprosy therefore of Naaman shall cleave unto thee, and unto thy seed for ever! And he went out from his presence a leper as white as snow."

Gehazi traded his employment as a servant of one of God's greatest prophets for a talent of silver, two changes of garments ... **and leprosy**. (SEE II KINGS, CHAPTER 5.)

Judas betrayed Jesus for thirty pieces of silver. That money cost Judas heaven, with its streets of gold and gates of pearl. What did the thirty pieces of silver buy for Judas? They bought his grave site, after he committed suicide. (SEE MATTHEW 27:3-8 AND ACTS 1:18.)

Pilate put his position as governor first. Pilate knew that Jesus was just, innocent, and falsely accused by envious religious leaders. Yet, Pilate put his desire to please people before pleasing God. (SEE MATTHEW 27:24 AND MARK 15:15.)

Can you even imagine what a different world we would live in today, if politicians desired to serve God more than to receive praise from the people? As for Pilate, he has all eternity to regret his fateful decision.

Demas put Christ first, as he ministered with the apostle Paul. His commitment lasted only for a short time. Paul wrote to Timothy: "Demas hath forsaken me, having loved this present world." II TIMOTHY 4:10

The "present world" that Demas made his priority is now buried under rubble and dirt. If Demas did not later repent of his sin of putting the world before Christ, his decision sealed his eternity. The Scriptures make this truth plain: "Ye adulterers and adulteresses, know ye not that the friendship of the world is enmity with God? whosoever therefore will be a friend of the world is the enemy of God. Love not the world, neither the things that are in the world. If any man love the world, the love of the Father is not in him." JAMES 4:4 AND I JOHN 2:15

One man, who was considering following Jesus, requested: "Lord, suffer me **first** to go and bury my father."

Jesus' answer probably shocked him. "Let the dead bury their dead: but go thou and preach the kingdom of God." MATTHEW 8:21-22

Jesus never compromised His demand that His followers put Him first.

Another man came to Jesus, and we can almost hear the excitement in his voice as he said: "Lord, I will follow thee; but let me **first go** bid them farewell, which are at home at my house."

And we can almost see his shoulders slump when Jesus answered: "No man, having put his hand to the plough, and looking back, is fit for the kingdom of God." (SEE LUKE 9:59-62.)

As Jesus prophesied of the closing days of time, He included a three-word warning to His followers: "**Remember Lot's wife**."

We follow His advice and pause to remember her. She fled from the raging fires of Sodom. Then her lust for her burning possessions and her concern for her dying family caused her to disobey the clear commandment of God. She had been warned not to look back. She looked back, and that one glance claimed her life.

God demands a whole-hearted forsaking of the world to put Him first. "Love not the world," He warns His people, "neither the things that are in the world. If any man love the world, the love of the Father is not in him. For all that is in the world, the lust of the flesh, and the lust of the eyes, and the pride of life, is not of the Father, but is of the world. And the world passeth away, and the lust thereof: but he that doeth the will of God abideth for ever."   I JOHN 2:15-17

If we are not willing to make Christ our priority in every area of our lives, we are not worthy to be His disciple.

Jesus clearly told us the qualifications that His disciples must meet: "If any man will come after me, let him deny himself, and take up his cross, and follow me. For whosoever will save his life shall lose it: and whosoever will lose his life for my sake shall find it.   For what is a man profited, if he shall gain the whole world, and lose his own soul?   or what shall a man give in exchange for his soul? He that loveth father or mother more than me is not worthy of me: and he that loveth son or daughter more than me is not worthy of me.   And he that taketh not his cross, and followeth after me, is not worthy of me.   He that findeth his life shall lose it: and he that loseth his life for my sake shall find it."   MATTHEW 16:24-26 + 10:37-39

We will *never* have financial peace of mind if our love for financial gain - or anything else or anyone else - comes before our love for God.   God must come first!   One who seeks wealth first will never accumulate enough to satisfy, for wealth will never satisfy the hunger and thirst of men.

Money does not give joy.

Money does not buy love.

Money cannot bring peace of mind.

Those who give their lives to obtain wealth will soon discover that its price is dissatisfaction. Greed continually lusts for more. Riches may buy pleasure for a season, but when the season ends, the emptiness and the longing for peace of mind will remain.

Jesus told us this parable: "The kingdom of heaven is like unto a merchant man, seeking goodly pearls: who, when he had found one pearl of great price, went and sold all that he had, and bought it." MATTHEW 13:45-46

The Pearl of great price is Jesus. Only when we are willing to forsake all else, are we able to have this One Eternal Pearl. There is a reason why Jesus chose the Pearl, rather than the most expensive jewel, the red diamond, to teach us a great truth.

The largest and most expensive pearl in the world was discovered about ten years ago by a Filipino fisherman. He found it in the sea, off the coast of the Palawan Island, in the Philippines. He did not find it in an oyster. No oyster could hold this pearl! It was twenty-six inches long by twelve inches wide and weighed nearly 75 pounds! He discovered this pearl in a giant clam, where pearls are rarely found.

The largest red diamond, the most expensive jewel in the world, has a value of eight million dollars.

The gigantic pearl the fisherman found has a value of one-hundred million dollars! Yet, that is not the reason Jesus compared Himself to the Pearl of great price. Men could discover a larger red diamond tomorrow, but it could *never* compare to the Pearl in the parable told by Jesus ... for the Pearl is the only jewel in the world to be born in and to grow in a living organism!

When we are born again, Jesus - the Pearl of great price - lives inside of us!

II Corinthians 4:6-7 shows us this beautiful truth: "For God, who commanded the light to shine out of darkness, hath shined in our hearts, to give the light of the knowledge of the glory of God in the face of Jesus Christ! But **we have this treasure in earthen vessels**, that the excellency of the power may be of God, and not of us!"

The pearl was born in and grew in the clam! Jesus, the priceless Pearl, the Treasure, lives within those who have been born again! His followers are His earthen vessels!

Lest we get proud, we need to remind ourselves that we can visit ***Joe Patty's*** restaurant in Pensacola, Florida, and purchase 12 oysters for $6.99! Or we can buy one dozen fresh clams online for $9.99!

It is not the vessel that holds the Pearl that is valuable! The Treasure is the Pearl in the clam!

The emphasis in both the world and the modern church today is to beautify and pamper the clam!

Back to the fisherman, the clam, and the 75-pound pearl... The fisherman, who considered the pearl to be his good luck charm, took it to his humble home and hid it under his bed. It remained there until catastrophe struck, and his home burned to the ground. The fisherman lost everything he owned ... ***except the pearl***.

A day is coming when catastrophe will strike, not just one home of one fisherman, but the entire earth.

II Peter 3:10 tells us: "... **the earth also and the works that are therein shall be burned up.**" All that man owns will be destroyed. The one priceless, eternal Jewel that will remain will be Jesus Christ. Those who have Him will need nothing else. II Corinthians 5:1 assures us: "... **if our earthly house of this tabernacle were dissolved**, we have a building of God, an house not made with hands, eternal in the heavens."

Everything in this world will burn. **When we have Jesus, our ETERNAL PEARL, we have ...**

> * **Our Savior.** MATTHEW 1:21
> * **Our Deliverer.** II TIMOTHY 4:18
> * **Our Healer.** ACTS 4:30
> * **Our Light.** JOHN 8:12
> * **Our Living Water.** JOHN 4:14
> * **Our Eternal Life.** I JOHN 5:11
> * **Our Resurrection.** JOHN 11:25-26
> * **Our Lord.** ROMANS 6:23
> * **Our Vine.** JOHN 15:4
> * **Our Hope.** I TIMOTHY 1:1
> * **Our Shepherd.** JOHN 10:14
> * **Our Gate to Heaven!** REVELATION 21:21

> "For __of__ him,
>
> and __through__ him,
>
> and __to__ him,
>
> are __all things:__
>
> *to whom be glory for ever.*
>
> **AMEN!"**
>
> Romans 11:36

How foolish it is to put the world and money, that is destined to burn, before Jesus, who offers eternal life and Heaven to all who put Him first!

God rebuked His people through His prophet, Haggai, for putting their houses before the house of God.

"Is it time for you, O ye," Haggai cried to the self-centered people of his day: "to dwell in your cieled houses, and this house lie waste? Now therefore thus saith the Lord of hosts; Consider your ways. Ye have sown much, and bring in little; ye eat, but ye have not enough; ye drink, but ye are not filled with drink; ye clothe you, but there is none warm; and he that earneth wages earneth wages to put it into a bag with holes. Thus saith the Lord of hosts; Consider your ways. Go up to the mountain, and bring wood, and build the house; and I will take pleasure in it, and I will be glorified, saith the Lord. Ye looked for much, and, lo it came to little; and when ye brought it home, I did blow upon it. Why? saith the Lord of hosts. Because of mine house that is waste, and ye run every man unto his own house." HAGGAI 1:4-9

God withheld His blessing upon His people because they put their needs before His. He put holes in their purses! He scattered their financial gain by blowing on it! Their money would not even provide for their needs!

Jesus said: "Therefore take no thought, saying, What shall we eat? or, What shall we drink? or, Wherewithal shall we be clothed? (For after all these things do the Gentiles seek:) for your heavenly Father knoweth that ye have need of all these things. But seek ye **FIRST** the kingdom of God, and his righteousness; and all these things shall be added unto you." MATTHEW 6:31-33

Do we obey His commandment? Are we really seeking Him first? Or are we no different than those who put fruit, soup, possessions, animals, raiment, houses, silver, and popularity before God?

We each need to examine our priorities. Where does God fit in? If He is not in first place, we are in direct disobedience to Him.

Does He come before our businesses, our jobs, our money, our families, our children, our friends, our houses, our education, our pleasures, our reputation ... our ALL?

Are we guilty of making the clam (ourselves) our priority? Or do we value the Pearl above all else?

Jesus asked us two questions in Matthew 16:26: "For what is a man profited, if he shall gain the whole world, and lose his own soul? or what shall a man give in exchange for his soul?"

As faithful followers of Jesus Christ, we all need to make every single decision based on this one question: "Am I putting God **first**?"

We will have peace of mind and contentment only by making Jesus our priority. Jesus spoke to us of the deceitfulness of riches. Men are deceived into believing that riches will satisfy and bring the longed-for financial peace of mind. However, no man has ever obtained peace of mind through his accumulation of riches.

God wants us to place all that we own and all that we hope to own in our hand. Then He wants us to lift our hand to Him, and allow Him to remove everything that He chooses to take. We must never close our hand into a fist of rebellion, but keep it always open and lifted to God. Trust Him to remove or add what He wants us to have.

Let us keep our eyes on Him, rather than fixing them on the possessions that remain in our hand.

We can never have peace of mind, unless the Prince of Peace reigns **first** in our lives.

Christ demands this commitment from each one of His followers.

STEP SEVEN

GOD IS OUR SOURCE

"Thus saith the Lord; Cursed be the man that trusteth in man, and maketh flesh his arm, and whose heart departeth from the Lord." JEREMIAH 17:5

Can a person possibly be under a curse from God and still have financial peace of mind?

God curses the man who trusts in himself and in other men, rather than in God! Until we put our trust firmly in God alone, rather than in ourselves, our education, our strength, our knowledge, our talents, our abilities, our employers, our business, our parents, our husband, our wife, our inheritance, our children, our bank accounts, our government, our pension, our retirement fund, our stocks and bonds, and our insurance policies, we will never find financial peace of mind!

God, and God alone, is our Source! All else can be taken away from us! Our strength can fade; our mind can deteriorate; our family can die; our employer can fire us;

our business can fail; our government can quit providing services; our bank can collapse; our pension may not be available when we need it; the stock market can crash; our insurance company can go bankrupt, our gold can be stolen; a storm or fire can take our home ... and the list of calamities could go on.

God, and God alone, will not - and cannot - fail. God promises us peace of mind only when we trust in Him.

"Thou wilt keep him in ***perfect peace, whose mind is stayed on thee***: because he trusteth in thee. Trust ye in the Lord for ever: for in the Lord Jehovah is everlasting strength." ISAIAH 26:3-4

God's Word is filled with His promises to care for us. The condition is that we place our trust wholly in Him. Jesus said: "Come unto me, all ye that labour and are heavy laden, and I will give you rest." MATTHEW 11:28

Rest is found only when we place our trust in God.

Jesus alone ***can*** and ***will*** give us rest. The rest He offers is a peace that comes only from Him. It can never come to the one whose trust is in man.

Can we safely put our trust in God? Will He provide for us?

Does He really care about our daily needs?

Listen to His answer to this question: "Behold the fowls of the air: for they sow not, neither do they reap, nor gather into barns; yet your heavenly Father feedeth them. Are ye not much better than they? ... why take ye thought for raiment? Consider the lilies of the field, how they grow;

they toil not, neither do they spin: and yet I say unto you, That even Solomon in all his glory was not arrayed like one of these. Wherefore, if God so clothe the grass of the field, which to day is, and to morrow is cast into the oven, shall he not much more clothe you, O ye of little faith?

"Therefore take no thought, saying, What shall we eat? or, What shall we drink? or, Wherewithal shall we be clothed ... for your heavenly Father knoweth that ye have need of all these things. But seek ye *first* the kingdom of God, and his righteousness; and all these things shall be added unto you. What man is there of you, whom if his son ask bread, will he give him a stone? Or if he ask a fish, will he give him a serpent? If ye then, being evil, know how to give good gifts unto your children, how much more shall your Father which is in heaven give good things to them that ask him?" MATTHEW 6:26 & 28-33 + 7:9-11

Does God care about man? Take a moment to reflect on His creation. He placed man in a perfect garden, furnished with colorful birds to sing to him; playful animals to give him pleasure; and flowers to perfume his air.

God has prepared man an even more luxurious place in heaven. We can only imagine its splendor, as we read His description of it.

Its gates are pearl; its streets gold; its walls of precious stones; its river as crystal; its trees always heavy with fruit.

Would our God, who began man's journey with the Garden of Eden and ends man's journey with Heaven, neglect caring for us in between the two?

God has given us a beautiful promise: "I will never leave thee, nor forsake thee." HEBREWS 13:5

The Bible says: "It is better to trust in the Lord than to put confidence in man. It is better to trust in the Lord than to put confidence in princes. Put not your trust in princes, nor in the son of man, in whom there is no help. Happy is he that hath the God of Jacob for his help, whose hope is in the Lord his God: which made heaven, and earth, the sea, and all that therein is: which keepeth truth for ever: which executeth judgment for the oppressed: which giveth food to the hungry. The Lord looseth the prisoners: the Lord openeth the eyes of the blind: the Lord raiseth them that are bowed down: the Lord loveth the righteous: the Lord preserveth the strangers; he relieveth the fatherless and widow: but the way of the wicked he turneth upside down." PSALMS 118:8-9 + 146:3 & 5-9

It is foolish to place our trust in man! God holds the life of man in *His* hand.

It is foolish to trust in our king or in our country's leaders, for God says: "The king's heart is in the hand of the Lord, as the rivers of water: he turneth it whithersoever he will." PROVERBS 21:1

The source of every single blessing is God. If man has blessed us, it is because God has put it in his heart to bless us! James 1:17 tells us: "*Every* good gift and every perfect gift is from above, and cometh down from the Father of lights!"

David was an elderly man, when he penned this truth: "I have been young, and now am old; yet have I not seen the righteous forsaken, nor his seed begging bread." PSALM 37:25

The Bible is filled with miraculous stories of God protecting His people and caring for their needs. We have God's promise that He does not change.

The same God who faithfully provided for His people yesterday still watches over us today!

Elijah was one of God's prophets who was faithfully cared for by his loving God. Jezebel had declared war on Elijah, vowing to kill him within twenty-four hours.

Elijah fled for his life into the wilderness, then sank exhausted under a juniper tree and begged God to let him die. As he lay under the tree, he prayed he would not wake up, and finally fell asleep. But God was not finished with Elijah's ministry on earth.

He sent an angel from heaven to cook and serve a meal to his weary prophet!

"And as he lay and slept under a juniper tree, behold, then an angel touched him, and said unto him, Arise and eat. And he looked, and, behold, there was a cake baken on the coals, and a cruse of water at his head. And he did eat and drink, and laid him down again. And the angel of the Lord came again the second time, and touched him, and said, Arise and eat; because the journey is too great for thee. And he arose, and did eat and drink, and went in the strength of that meat forty days and forty nights!" I KINGS 19:5-8

Elijah was not the only servant of God who was cared for by angels. God said of His angels: "Are they not all ministering spirits, sent forth to minister for them who shall be heirs of salvation?" HEBREWS 1:14

Jesus warned us to never offend a child or a new believer: "Take heed that ye despise not one of these little ones; for I say unto you, That in heaven ***their angels*** do always behold the face of my Father which is in heaven." MATTHEW 18:10

An angel has been given to each of God's people to minister to his needs! Psalm 91:11 is a beautiful promise: "He shall give his angels charge over thee, to keep thee in all thy ways."

It was Elisha, Elijah's successor, who was with a group of workers, putting an addition on the house for the prophets. One man had borrowed an axe head. As the timber fell, the axe head fell into the river. The man cried to Elisha: "Alas, master! for it was borrowed!" Elisha served and knew his God. He calmly asked where it happened. He then cut down a stick and threw it at the place it fell. The last four words of II Kings 6:6 reveal that God cares about the smallest things that worry us and rob us of peace.

"And the iron did swim."

Does God still take care of His people?

Meet John Craig!

John Craig was arrested during the Inquisition and ultimately scheduled for execution. John escaped the night before he was to be executed. He fled through the Italian back country, running until he could run no longer.

No strength remained in him, for his food was gone. He had no money.

As if he did not have enough trouble, a dog approached him.

John tried repeatedly to drive it away, with no success. The dog kept coming back.

Although John did not realize it until later, that dog was on a mission from God and was determined to accomplish it. John finally gave up trying to drive the dog away.

The dog approached him again, and this time, he completed his mission. He opened his mouth and laid a purse at John's feet. Then the dog left.

John opened the purse. Inside was enough money to finance the rest of his trip to freedom!

Then there was John Brenz, a friend of Martin Luther, who was marked for assassination by Emperor Charles V.

John escaped the Spanish Cavalry by running into a neighbor's hayloft.

He had only one loaf of bread with him.

Then a hen paid him a visit, laid an egg beside him, and left. John welcomed his faithful visitor each day for fourteen days.

Then, to his dismay, on the fifteenth day of his exile, the hen failed to deliver an egg.

Both the hen and John's peace of mind were gone. He was left with one question: "What am I going to do without the hen?"

Shouts from the street below interrupted his worries: "The cavalrymen are gone at last!"

The hen knew before John did that her catering services were no longer needed.

The dog ... the hen ... and *a spider?*

Robert Bruce of Scotland was running from his persecutors, when he saw a small cave and ran into it. Right behind him came ... a ***spider***.

Robert watched the spider spin a web over the cave opening. He was fascinated at the amazing speed of the spider. The industrious spider continued to almost frantically spin, until the web entirely covered the cave opening in mere seconds.

Robert was pondering the work of the spider, when he heard men approaching the cave.

One called to the others: "There is no use looking in this cave. If Robert had run in here, he would have broken that spider web!"

Robert Bruce later wrote about the spider and his own prayer of thanksgiving: "O God, I thank Thee that in the tiny bowels of a spider, You can place for me a shelter!"

Dare we not trust such a God, who can send ...
- Ravens to cater food.
- A fish to deliver a coin to a fisherman.

- An abundance of oil in one small pot.
- And cause an iron axe head to swim!

Our God – our Refuge – our Provider – has no limitations! When our God gets involved …

- donkeys talk;
- walls fall;
- fish deliver;
- ravens cater;
- angels protect;
- devils flee;
- seas and rivers part;
- whales swallow – and vomit;
- chains fall;
- iron gates open;
- iron swims;
- diseases leave;
- chariots of fire pulled by horses of fire descend;
- Jesus ascends;
- horses and chariots of fire surround;
- fires lose their power to burn;
- the mouths of lions close;
- doors shut;
- doors open;
- angels bake;

- tombs empty;
- hens lay;
- dogs finance;
- spiders spin;

... and we could fill not just pages, but books, telling the wonders of our Lord! John finally closed his book by writing: "And there are also many other things which Jesus did, the which, if they should be written every one, I suppose that even the world itself could not contain the books that should be written!" His last word was a heartfelt shout that still rings down through the centuries to our day: "AMEN"!

AMEN is the last word of the book of John and it is the last word in the Bible! **AMEN** is a victorious shout of assurance that we can trust all that has been said! It is **truth**! It is **certain**!

We can stake our lives and our eternal souls on the Word of God, for it is forever TRUTH!

Stop worrying!

Put your trust in God!

He "openeth, and no man shutteth; and shutteth, and no man openeth!"

Trust the One, who said to His church:

"I know thy works: behold, I have set before thee an open door, and no man can shut it: for thou hast a little strength, and hast kept my word, and hast not denied my name." REVELATION 3:7-8

> Jesus knew *their works!*
> His servants had *a little strength!*
> **His servants had *kept His Word!***
> His servants had *not denied His name!*

Our faithful LORD responded to the faithfulness of His servants, by setting an open door before them ... a door that no man, no beast, no devil could shut! Why? Because JESUS IS THE DOOR!   (SEE JOHN 10:7 & 9.)

How must our Father feel, when we, who are His children, cannot trust such a God as this?

God has promised His people food during famine and protection in the midst of war!

"Behold, the eye of the Lord is upon them that fear him, upon them that hope in his mercy; to deliver their soul from death, and to keep them alive in famine. Our soul waiteth for the Lord: he is our help and our shield. For our heart shall rejoice in him, *because we have trusted in his holy name*." PSALM 33:18-21

Our bodies may die, but God delivers our souls from eternal death!

What man or government can make these promises?

Do you believe that God is God and that He is able to keep His people alive in the midst of a famine?

We serve the God who fed the children of Israel daily by raining manna from heaven!

We serve the God who poured water from a dry rock for His thirsty children!

We serve the God who kept clothes and shoes from wearing out during a forty-year hike in the wilderness!

We serve the God who sent clouds of quails!

We serve the God who commanded ravens to cater bread and meat every morning and evening to Elijah, His faithful prophet!

We serve the God who continually filled a widow's barrel with meal and cruse with oil during a drought, so she, her son, and His prophet could eat!

We serve the God who fed thousands of hungry people by simply multiplying a lad's small lunch!

We serve the God who sent a fish to pick up money in its mouth and then to swim to Peter's fishhook, so taxes could be paid!

We serve the God who filled enough vessels with oil from one small pot, so a widow could sell the oil to pay off her creditors!

We serve the God who turned water into wine for an embarrassed host at a wedding!

What man or king can dispatch angels; command birds to cater food; rain bread from heaven; make wine out of water; command a fish to do his bidding; multiply food to feed a multitude of hungry people; fill empty nets with fish for fishermen, or cause waters like rivers to stream out of a rock? It was God who "... brought streams also out of the rock, and caused waters to run down like rivers!" PSALM 78:16

How foolish to trust in man when the awesome Creator of the universe promises to care for all who put their trust in Him!

Jesus had finished His ministry on earth. He had been crucified, buried, and had risen from death. Before He ascended to Heaven's throne, He knelt on the shore of the sea of Tiberias and built a fire of coals. He then cooked a meal of fish and bread for His disciples. Can you hear His joyful invitation to them, as He called: "**Come and dine**!" (SEE JOHN 21:9-13.)

Jesus not only prepared a meal for men that day, He served it to them!

He still serves His people today!

He prepares a banquet of blessings for His children. Can you see the love radiating from His face? Can you hear the joy in His voice, as He calls to you: "**Come and dine**!"

Our great God, who holds all creation in His hand, is concerned about His children's every need. What man do you know who is concerned for the welfare of a sparrow? God cares!

Jesus said: "Are not two sparrows sold for a farthing? and one of them shall not fall on the ground without your Father. But the very hairs of your head are all numbered. Fear ye not therefore, ye are of more value than many sparrows." MATTHEW 10:29-31

Men regard sparrows as nearly worthless. Ten sparrows were sold for one Roman penny when Jesus walked the earth. If God watches over the least of the birds, how much more will He watch over you? He is the One who said that you are worth far more than many sparrows!

Which of your friends know how many hairs you have on your head? **God knows**! God wants you to come to Him with your needs.

Jesus instructed us to pray: *"Give us this day our daily bread."*

He wrote His invitation to you in I Peter 5:7: *"Casting all your cares upon Him; for He careth for you."*

GOD IS OUR SOURCE!

We should *never* place our trust in *anything or anyone* else! Jesus said: "Children, how hard is it for them that trust in riches to enter into the kingdom of God!" MARK 10:24

God warned: "He that trusteth in his riches shall fall!" PROVERBS 11:28

"Charge them that are rich in this world, that they be not highminded, *nor trust in uncertain riches*, but in the living God, who giveth us richly all things to enjoy." I TIMOTHY 6:17

God demands trust from His people. Trust means *to commit to one's care for use or safekeeping*. How can we say we trust our souls and our everlasting destiny to God, when we are afraid to even trust our lives here on earth to Him?

How can we say we believe that God will safely guard our soul, when we do not believe He can even provide a meal for us? Has not our God proven time and time again that He is a Father who can be trusted to care for His children? We grieve Him when we fail to trust Him for our needs.

God's children claim to trust Him. But do we trust Him enough to completely put our lives in His hands?

There was a famous tightrope walker named Blondin, who performed daring feats to cheering crowds in the 1890s.

Blondin strung a tightrope across Niagara Falls. Then, before 10,000 screaming people, he inched his way from the Canadian side of the Falls to the United States side. When he reached the United States, the crowd began shouting his name:

"Blondin! Blondin! Blondin! Blondin!"

Finally, he raised his arms to quiet the crowd and shouted to them: "I am Blondin! Do you believe in me?"

The crowd shouted back:

"We believe! We believe! We believe!"

Again, Blondin quieted the crowd, and this time he shouted to them: "I am going back across the tightrope! This time I am going to carry someone on my back! Do you believe I can do that?"

The crowd responded with a mighty chant: "We believe! We believe!"

Blondin quieted them one more time, and then asked: "Who will be that person?"

The crowd instantly became deathly silent. Finally, out of the huge crowd, stepped one man.

He climbed on Blondin's shoulders, and for the next three and one-half hours, Blondin inched his way back across the tightrope to the Canadian side of the Falls.

Ten-thousand people roared: "We believe! We believe!"

But only one person really believed.

Jesus longs for us to believe in Him and trust Him with all our hearts.

He looked upon Jerusalem, a city inhabited by God's chosen people, and cried: "O Jerusalem, Jerusalem, thou that killest the prophets, and stonest them which are sent unto thee, how often would I have gathered thy children together, even as a hen gathereth her chickens under her wings, and ye would not!" MATTHEW 23:37

A fire raged through a farmer's barn. When the fire had finished its devastating work, he and his neighbor walked among the destruction. His animals were burned beyond recognition.

Suddenly, in amazement, they heard the sound of life. Tracing its source, they discovered baby chicks that had taken refuge underneath the feathers of their charred mother.

"I would have gathered thy children together, even as a hen gathers her chickens under her wings."

The hen gave her life as a covering for her chicks. Jesus gave His blood as a covering for our sins. How can we ever doubt His love and promises to care for us?

There is a place of protection in God that shields His children from destruction.

Psalm 91:1 says: "He that dwelleth in the secret place of the most High shall abide under the shadow of the Almighty."

King David took shelter there. He cried out to God: "Hide me under the shadow of thy wings." PSALM 17:8

God has a promise for all who come to Him. "He shall cover thee with his feathers, and under his wings shalt thou trust." PSALM 91:4

Have *you* taken shelter there? God spoke these words of blessing through Moses:

"The eternal God is thy refuge, and underneath are the everlasting arms." DEUTERONOMY 33:27

Are *you* trusting in mortal man or the eternal God who lovingly holds His children in His everlasting arms?

God sets before every man a blessing and a curse. He leaves the choice of which one we will receive to us. If we do not choose the blessing, we will receive the curse.

THE CURSE

"Thus saith the Lord; Cursed be the man that trusteth in man, and maketh flesh his arm, and whose heart departeth from the Lord." JEREMIAH 17:5

THE BLESSING

"Blessed is the man that trusteth in the Lord, and whose hope the Lord is." JEREMIAH 17:7

If we choose to place our trust in money, ourselves, men, our government, or anything in this world, we will *never* have financial peace of mind. Instead, a curse from God Himself will be upon us.

Only by trusting in our Creator will we have God's blessing.

With His blessing, comes financial peace of mind.

We repeat this beautiful promise.

Engrave it in your heart!

"Thou wilt keep him in perfect peace, whose mind is stayed on thee: because he trusteth in thee."

ISAIAH 26:3

CONCLUSION

During times of economic distress or personal tragedies, many lose their jobs, their incomes, their savings, their financial security, and their hope for their future.

We must adhere to God's principles in order to survive.

Are you keeping the principles discussed in this book?

The question is not whether or not you **believe** these principles. The question is whether or not you are putting each one of them into **practice** in your life?

Let's look at these seven steps again. This time, examine your heart and your life.

Step 1: Work 6 Days! Rest One!

Even if we are without a job, the very worst thing we can do is **nothing**. It is no disgrace for a lawyer or a school teacher to shovel snow, rake yards, clean houses, or volunteer to work in a worthwhile organization. The Son of God labored as a carpenter! Sitting home brooding will never improve your situation! (SEE MARK 6:3.)

Step 2: Thanks for the Fish!

Are you thankful for what you *do* have? Begin right now to thank God for His blessings! "Let every thing that hath breath praise the Lord. Praise ye the Lord!" PSALM 150:6

Step 3: Don't Covet!

"Let your conversation be without covetousness; and be content with such things as ye have: for he hath said, I will never leave thee, nor forsake thee. So that we may boldly say, The Lord is my helper, and I will not fear what man shall do unto me. And having food and raiment let us be therewith content." HEBREWS 13:5-6 AND I TIMOTHY 6:8

Step 4: Be Honest!

Are you honest in all of your financial and business dealings? Do you need to make restitution to anyone?

Step 5: Give!

You may think that you have nothing to give, but you do. Give someone a helping hand, an encouraging word, a genuine smile, a heart of love, your time in prayer for their needs.

There are many who are going through hard times. Your attitude toward your situation can give others the will to go on.

Step 6: Put God First!

Are you putting God first in your life ... in *all* things?

Step 7: Trust God!

If we look at ourselves and at our situation, we will have fear. We know that we are not able to prevent disasters and tragedies from striking our nation, city, home, or body.

We must look to God for our needs, for He alone is all powerful. He tells us to: "Arise, shine: for thy light is come, and the glory of the Lord is risen upon thee! For, behold, the darkness shall cover the earth, and gross darkness the people: but the Lord shall arise upon thee, and His glory shall be seen upon thee!" ISAIAH 60:1-2

Jesus left us these powerful words to live by when the storms of life rage about us. Study them carefully – and prayerfully!

"Therefore **whosoever heareth these sayings of mine, and doeth them**, I will liken him unto a wise man, which built his house upon a rock: and the rain descended, and the floods came, and the winds blew, and beat upon that house; and it fell not: for it was founded upon a rock. And **every one that heareth these sayings of mine, and doeth them not**, shall be likened unto a foolish man, which built his house upon the sand: and the rain descended, and the floods came, and the winds blew, and beat upon that house; and it fell: and great was the fall of it." MATTHEW 7:24-27

The house that Jesus is referring to is our life, not a structure of wood or bricks. We learn in His parable, that both the wise and the foolish heard the words of Jesus.

The foolish ignored His words and lived by their own rules. Jesus said of their house: "Great was the fall of it."

The fall of the foolish will end in hell itself.

The time to make a wise choice is on this side of eternity. God's mercy is extended to each one of us. His mercy is seen in the form of a cross, on which He allowed His beloved and only begotten Son to be tortured and die … for us.

Receive Jesus as your Savior today.

Then your victorious shout can be Psalm 86:12-13:

> "I will praise thee, O Lord my God, with all my heart:
> and I will glorify thy name for evermore.
> For great is thy mercy toward me:
> and **thou hast delivered my soul from the lowest hell**."

The wise not only *heard* the words of Jesus, but they *lived* by them.

Jesus said in Luke 4:4: "Man shall not **live** by bread alone, but **by every word of God**."

Rain will pour and winds will howl on both the wise and the foolish.

There is no man who will escape the storms of life.

Some people are swept away in a storm. Only those, who are founded upon the Rock, Jesus Christ, the Son of the living God, will still be standing when the storms cease.

The same flood that destroyed the wicked, also lifted the ark that enclosed Noah and his family.

- **The wicked drowned in the flood.**

- **Noah and his family were lifted up to higher ground - above the highest mountains -** *by the same flood waters!*

One family of eight, who had lived in obedience to God, was still standing when the winds ceased, the flood waters abated, and the sun shone again.

A powerful storm raged across America from 1929 to 1939. We call it *"The Great Depression"*.

Many, including faithful church goers, were not sitting in heavenly places with Jesus when the thunders crashed and the economy collapsed. They had built their houses on the shifting sands of money.

The winds raged upon both the foolish and the wise, stripping them of their wealth, jobs, and possessions. The wise do not escape the storms of life! The Bible tells us: "To every thing there is a season, and a time to every purpose under the heaven: a time to be born, and a time to die; a time to plant, and a time to pluck up that which is planted ... **a**

time to get, and a time to lose; a time to keep, and a time to cast away." ECCLESIASTES 3:1-2 & 6

As surely as there is a time for each of us to be born and to die, there will also be times of getting and times of losing.

In 1931 alone, 20,000 men in the United States committed suicide. In a frantic effort to stem the tide of suicides, doctors prescribed opiates.

Rather than running to the Rock for protection, husbands and fathers devastated their families, by instead choosing death or addictions.

The foundation of money is shifting sand. When the storm comes, those who rest their lives on money will be swept away in the flood waters.

The Lord gave us only two choices:

1. Build our lives on Jesus, the only sure Foundation.

2. Build our lives on this earth, that is destined to burn.

I Corinthians 3:11 insures us that there is only one Foundation that can promise us safety when the storms rage. Man cannot lay this Foundation. God has already laid it for us. He simply invites each one of us to build our lives on the Foundation He has provided.

"For other foundation can no man lay than that is laid, which is Jesus Christ." I CORINTHIANS 3:11

Only the wise will heed His counsel and build their lives upon Jesus. ***Will you be one?***

Our Prayer is that

JESUS,

God's only begotten Son, the Prince of Peace, will bless you with His peace, as you not only hear, but live by each one of God's seven steps to financial peace of mind.

A Final Word ...

Job, a wealthy man of old, lost not only all his riches overnight, but also his seven sons and three daughters.

His response to this devastating storm still stands shining in the book that bears his name:

"Naked came I out of my mother's womb, and naked shall I return thither: the Lord gave, and the Lord hath taken away; blessed be the name of the Lord."   JOB 1:21

When death takes us from this world, we leave with empty hands.

It is said that we never see a hearse towing a trailer.

God's Word says it this way: "We brought nothing into this world, and it is certain we can carry nothing out." I TIMOTHY 6:7

The only possession that will mean anything to us, as we begin our first ten million years of eternity, will be our Savior and our Lord, Jesus Christ, the Pearl of great price.

He alone is our Ark of Safety.

If you do not have Jesus, you have nothing.

If you have Jesus, you have everything.   Having Him live in your heart insures you of an eternal home in Heaven.

There will be no financial problems in Heaven.

Streets will not be paved with asphalt, but with pure gold!

Gates will not be made of iron, but of Pearl!

There will be no ghettos, but mansions.

Jewels, not bricks, will adorn Heaven's foundations and walls!

Jesus told us: "Lay not up for yourselves treasures upon earth, where moth and rust doth corrupt, and where thieves break through and steal: but lay up for yourselves treasures in heaven, where neither moth nor rust doth corrupt, and where thieves do not break through nor steal." MATTHEW 6:19-20

The apostle Paul wrote: "Seek those things which are above, where Christ sitteth on the right hand of God. Set your affection on things above, not on things on the earth." COLOSSIANS 3:1-2

There is a better day coming! In fact, God promised us: "Eye hath not seen, nor ear heard, neither have entered into the heart of man, the things which God hath prepared for them that love him!" I CORINTHIANS 2:9

God sent Jesus from Heaven to save us.

If you want to receive Jesus, talk to Him now.

Confess that you are a sinner.

Realize that you are without hope.

Admit that you have done nothing to deserve Heaven.

Every sinner is destined to eternal death in hell.

We are *all* included in this death sentence!

Thank Jesus for taking your sentence of death and suffering in your place! He paid for your sins!

Receive His priceless Gift of salvation!

Thank Him again! He allowed His blood to flow from His tortured body for one reason: **He loves you**.

Receive Him, not only as your Savior, but as your Lord. Give Him total control of your new life. When you submit to Him as Lord, you will become His willing servant.

Ask Him for His power and His help in your new life. Die to your old life! Go with Christ to His cross, and crucify your old man of sin. Go with Christ to His tomb! Bury your old man of sin in the waters of baptism.

Then be resurrected with Christ! Give Christ total control of your life! Let Him live His life through you, speak His words through you, and do His works through you!

Trust the Lord! Let Him lead, as you follow! Ask Him for His wisdom in every decision you make. Put Him in complete charge of every detail of your new life.

Consult His Word! Obey His commandments! He is as close to you as just one prayer!

God, who is in charge of all creation, can, and will, take good care of you. He simply wants you to let Him do it!

"I am crucified with Christ: nevertheless I live; yet not I, but **Christ liveth in me**: and the life which I now live in the flesh I live by the faith of the Son of God, who **loved <u>me</u>**, and **gave himself for <u>me</u>**." Galatians 2:20

"That he would grant you, according to the riches of his glory, to be strengthened with might by his Spirit in the inner man; that **Christ may dwell in your hearts by faith**." Ephesians 3:16-17

"Therefore we are buried with him by baptism into death: that like as Christ was raised up from the dead by the glory of the Father, even so we also should walk in newness of life. For if we have been planted together in the likeness of his death, we shall be also in the likeness of his resurrection: knowing this, that our old man is crucified with him, that the body of sin might be destroyed, that henceforth we should not serve sin. For he that is dead is freed from sin." Romans 6:4-7

"Therefore if any man be in Christ, he is a new creature: old things are passed away; behold, all things are become new." II Corinthians 5:17

"Unto him that loved us, and washed us from our sins in his own blood, and hath made us kings and priests unto God and his Father; to him be glory and dominion for ever and ever. **AMEN**." REVELATION 1:5-6

3

Practical Steps to Get Out of Debt ... and They Work!

If you are in debt, and if you live by each one of these Seven Biblical Principles, then _you_ can get out of debt in just three steps.

It is easy to fall into debt.

It is harder to climb out.

If you plan to be out of debt someday, you must begin to climb. You can be out of debt much sooner than you think. Simply follow these three steps.

Step 1: Cancel your credit cards.
Step 2: Follow this Step to Pay Your Bills.
Step 3: Follow this Step to Pay Your Mortgage.

1
CANCEL YOUR CREDIT CARDS

The average American now has personal debt that is over $38,000. This amount does not include home mortgages. Twenty percent of Americans must set aside 50% to 100% of their income toward debt repayment.

In the 1950's, Americans saved $8 out of every $100 earned. Today, the average saving is $1 per $100. Why are Americans no longer saving for emergencies? Could it be because that in just the past six years, credit card debt has nearly tripled?

TED BEGINS HIS CLIMB OUT OF DEBT

We are going to look at Ted's financial condition. Ted is 38 years old. He thought he would be in much better financial condition at this age than he is. He has always had a job. He has always paid his bills on time. However, no matter how much Ted works and how responsible he is about paying his bills, his financial condition never seems to improve.

Ted needed an extra incentive to get out of debt - and a plan that would work.

When he read these three steps, he knew this was the plan for him. He was ready to begin his climb out of debt.

Ted studied **Step One**. He was shocked to learn how much money his credit cards were costing him.

Ted was actually in better financial condition than many Americans. He had two credit cards. One had a $7,500 balance, and the second had a $900 balance.

The interest rate of 15% was accumulating daily. He had decided a few months earlier not to charge anything to his credit cards. He paid the minimum payment on the due date each month. He waited to get his credit cards paid . . . *and he waited . . . and he waited.*

Ted was shocked to realize that he would wait *24 years* to pay off the credit card with the $7,500 balance!

Listed below are some things that Ted learned about this one credit card:

He will be 62 years old when he finally achieves a zero balance.

He will pay $7,258 for interest charges alone.

He will pay $98.50 for his $50 shoes.

His $38 dinner will cost him $74.86.

He had complained at the gas station when he paid $2.50 a gallon for gas. It would end up costing him $4.93 a gallon!

He had charged his $1,200 forty-two-inch plasma television set. Its final price would grow to $2,364! Ted would still be paying for his outdated model, while wishing he could afford a newer one.

These figures hold true only because Ted would pay his minimum payment on time every month. If he had been penalized even once for being late with a payment or going over his debt limit, his cost would escalate, and his interest rate would be raised substantially. If he had continued to put charges on the card, he would have signed himself up for an entire lifetime of debt. If he had a credit card with a variable *(changeable)* interest rate, the cost of charging would have risen with every raise in the federal interest rate.

Ted could have reduced his interest costs considerably if he had paid a regular monthly payment of $187.50 instead of paying only the minimum payment that was due.

Ted still would pay:
    $3.48 for his $2.50 gallon of gas.
    $69.50 for his $50 shoes.
    $52.82 for his $38 meal.
    $1,668 for his $1,200 television set!
    Monthly payments of $187.50 for nearly 5 years.
    Nearly $3,000 in interest alone.

When Ted realized how much his credit cards were costing him, he had his incentive to begin his first step. He decided he would not spend countless days of his lifetime enriching credit card companies.

He looked again at **1*: cancel your credit cards***. This first step is the hardest step for most Americans. The only way Ted could have skipped this step is if he paid his credit card balance in full every month. Ted couldn't afford to pay off his credit cards, so he canceled them.

He had thought it would be hard, but when he realized how much they were costing him, he enjoyed canceling them!

(Note: If you simply cannot bring yourself to rid yourself of all credit cards, keep one locked up at home. Do not take it with you when you leave the house. Do not charge over the telephone or Internet. In other words, don't use it!)

2
CHANGE YOUR THINKING

Ted listed all his bills. He wrote down his monthly payments and the balance owed to pay each one in full.

He wrote his bills on a chart, listing the one with the highest balance on top and the one with the lowest balance on the bottom. His total debts discouraged him. He didn't know that his list looked much better than the average American's list. The average price for new and existing houses in the nation's 32 largest metropolitan areas was $309,200 in June of 2005. It has risen since then - and so have the mortgages!

TED'S LIST OF BILLS

BILL	BALANCE DUE	MONTHLY PAYMENT
Mortgage	$150,000.00	$900.00
Automobile	$12,000.00	$315.00
Credit Card 1	$7,500.00	$188.00
Credit Card 2	$900.00	$75.00
Total	$170,400.00	$1,478.00

In the future, Ted would think of his car debt, his mortgage debt and his credit card debt as one debt with a total balance of $170,400.00. He would think of his monthly payments as one monthly payment of $1,478.00, rather than four separate monthly payments.

Ted looked at his income. How much could he afford to pay on his $170,400 debt?

If his answer had been less than $1,478.00, Ted would have been in serious trouble. He would have had to increase his income. He could have looked around his home, garage, and yard to see if he had anything he could sell. He would have needed to take a good long look at his spending habits.

Where could he reduce his expenditures? How could he increase his income? Could he mow lawns or shovel snow to earn extra money? Perhaps he even needed to sell his house and move into a smaller one. At this point, he could have become angry, blaming God, his boss, his wife, or the world for the financial crisis he is facing. Or Ted could bow his head and simply ask the Lord for wisdom.

God is in the business of leading His children, helping them, and giving them knowledge and ideas.

God doesn't want His children to be burdened under a mountain of debt!

Ted could open his Bible and not only read, but *believe* God's promises in Proverbs 3:5-7:

> "Trust in the LORD with all thine heart; and lean not unto thine own understanding.
>
> In *all thy ways* acknowledge *(recognize)* him, and he shall direct thy paths.
>
> Be not wise in thine own eyes."

Ted could recognize his need for the wisdom of God, not just in his spiritual walk, but in his finances. He remembered God's promise in James 1:5:

> "If any of you lack wisdom,
>
> let him ask of God,
>
> that giveth to all men liberally,
>
> and upbraideth *(scolds)* not;
>
> and it shall be given him."

Ted bowed his head, and simply asked God for His help. Then he checked his monthly budget to see how he could reduce his spending habits. After checking and rechecking his figures, Ted realized that he was wasting money on things he didn't need. He could save enough to pay $1,750 a month to reduce his debt. That was $272 more than the $1,478 he had been paying!

Ted looked at the chart he made. He would apply this $272 extra to his lowest bill, Credit Card Two. Instead of paying the $75 payment that was due, Ted would add the $272 to the $75 and pay $347 on this balance.

Credit card Two would be completely paid off in less than three months!

Ted followed his plan, and just over two months later, Ted drew a line through Credit Card Two. It was paid in full.

Now Ted had $347 extra a month to put on his debts. He applied the extra he had to Credit Card One. Instead of paying the $188 payment that was due, he added $347 to his $188 payment on Credit Card One. He would now be paying $535 on this bill!

Just over fourteen months later, Ted drew a line through Credit Card One! He had eliminated another bill!

Instead of making payments on his two cards for over 25 years, he eliminated both of them in a year and a half!

Ted not only began his climb, he disciplined himself to follow his plan. He didn't spend the money that he was no longer paying on credit cards.

He had changed his thinking.

He had one big bill - and one big payment.

His payment was still $1,750 in Ted's mind, even though two bills had been eliminated.

Ted continued to pay his monthly payment of $1,750 on his total debt. He added his extra $535 to his $315 car payment and began to pay $850 each month on his automobile. In about 15 months, Ted's car loan was paid in full!

Ted had one bill left - his dreaded mortgage. Instead of paying $900 per month, he would now pay $1,750 a month. The next step would show Ted exactly how to do this, so his mortgage would be reduced the quickest way.

Ted has completed 1 and 2. He was now ready to begin 3 and complete his steady climb out of the pit of debt.

3

PAY YOUR MORTGAGE

Ted's house cost him $190,000.

He paid a down payment of $40,000.

He was left with a mortgage of $150,000, financed at 6 % interest.

If Ted faithfully paid his payment of $900 each month - on time - he would pay $323,319 for his house.

The interest Ted paid to his lending institution would cost him $173,319.00.

He did not want to give nearly $174,000 to his mortgage holder! Was there a way to keep from paying all of this, besides selling his house and moving into a tent?

Ted studied Step 3.

Ted had followed Steps One and Two. He now had $1,750 a month to pay on his mortgage. He had $850 extra to add to his monthly payment of $900!

Ted could pay $850 extra a month a right way or a wrong way. By paying it the right way, Ted would know within a few dollars exactly what he owed on his house each month. He was like most people. He had no idea what his principal balance was or even how to calculate what it should be. He would need to call his lender to find out what his balance was. He would have to trust that he was being told the truth.

Ted realized his first step was to obtain an Amortization Schedule. That would be easy. He would ask his bank for one. He was shocked when his banker refused to give him one. He offered to buy one but was told providing one for him was against bank policy. Ted's sister helped him out by using the Internet. Ted had his Amortization Schedule in no time, costing him only a few sheets of paper and his sister about five minutes.

He couldn't believe the figures on his Amortization Schedule. Ted studied the figures for the first year. They showed exactly what portions of Ted's payment would go to paying his lender and what portion would actually reduce the amount he owed. The Principal column showed what was actually being deducted from the balance of his loan each month.

TED'S AMORTIZATION SCHEDULE

MONTH DUE	PAYMENT	INTEREST	PRINCIPAL	BALANCE DUE
January	$900	$750	$150	$149,850
February	$900	$749	$151	$149,699
March	$900	$748	$152	$149,547
April	$900	$748	$152	$149,395
May	$900	$747	$153	$149,242
June	$900	$746	$154	$149,088
July	$900	$745	$155	$148,933
August	$900	$745	$155	$148,778
September	$900	$744	$156	$148,622
October	$900	$743	$157	$148,465
November	$900	$742	$158	$148,307
December	$900	$742	$158	$148,149

After Ted paid a total of $10,800.00 the first year, his loan would only be reduced by $1,851.00. Ted and his house would both be worn out by the time his mortgage was paid! How would he even afford to keep it in good repair? He sighed, thinking: "This third step had better work!"

Ted would apply his $850.00 extra a month to his loan. He sat down with his amortization schedule, his calculator, a pen, his check book and his extra $850.00 to figure out exactly how much he would pay on or before his payment due date.

He wrote down $1,750 at the top of his paper.

He subtracted his $900 payment. He crossed out the entire line of January. It was now paid in full.

Ted looked at his February line. The principal payment due was $151. He subtracted $151 from the $850 balance he had left of his payment. Ted crossed out the entire month of February - all the way across! Ted would *never* have to pay the $749 interest due in February! By adding $151 to his payment, he had just saved $749!

For the first time since he began to study Step Three, Ted found himself grinning.

He still had $699 left of his payment. He subtracted his March principal of $152 from the balance he had left to pay. He then crossed out his March payment - all the way across. He would *never* pay the $748 interest charged him in March!

He still had $547 left.

He subtracted his April principal amount of $152 and crossed out April. Ted was beginning to have fun. He had $395 left. He subtracted $153 and crossed out May. An extra $154 took care of June. He looked at July - he needed another $67 to cross out July too! He didn't have quite enough money in his budget to pay another principal payment. He could either keep it and add it to next month's total payment, or … "Annie, do you have $67 stashed away anyplace? Could you give up some of those state quarters?"

She handed him $67.00 and Ted crossed out July.

His paper now looked like this:

Month	Principal Amount	Remaining Balance
		$1,750.00
January	~~$900.00~~	~~$850.00~~
February	~~$151.00~~	~~$699.00~~
March	~~$152.00~~	~~$547.00~~
April	~~$152.00~~	~~$395.00~~
May	~~$153.00~~	~~$242.00~~
June	~~$154.00~~	~~$88.00~~
July	~~$155.00~~	~~($67.00)~~

He paid $917 extra on his payment in January and eliminated six months of interest charges. Ted would never pay $4,483.00 in interest charges.

He also knew with this method of payments exactly what he owed. He owed $148,933 at the end of July.

When Ted paid his payment, he wrote this message on both his check and an enclosed note:

"The $917.00 extra is to be applied to the Principal Balance *ONLY!*"

Ted's lender did not like what Ted was doing. So he simply ignored Ted's message on his check and applied the extra money Ted sent in a less costly way to him.

Ted knew that this may happen. He allowed his lender time to post the payment, then he called and asked for the balance due on his loan. He checked the figures. They didn't even begin to match! Ted asked if the extra money he put on his loan was applied in full to his principal balance. He listened to music while he was being transferred to someone who could help him. Finally, he was referred to someone who could answer his question.

"Did you want all of the extra money you sent applied to the principal?"

"Yes. I wrote you a note and also wrote a message on my check telling you how to apply it."

"Yes."

"Did you apply it in that way?"

"No."

Will you?"

"Yes!"

Ted's February payment came due. Even though his Amortization Schedule showed that the next payment he would make would be his August payment, Ted knew he had to pay his payment on the due date of *every single month*. The extra he had paid in January had been applied to the principal due, and was not a payment being made early. Ted got out his Amortization Schedule and wrote February in the margin by his August payment. He was anxious to see how much he could save by paying his extra $850.00 this month.

Ted first crossed out the payment due in August.

Then he added the Principal balances due in September, October, November, December and January.

He needed an extra $95.00 to get rid of February's payment. He knew his wife had some money left over from her garage sale.

"Annie!"

"How much?"

"$95 will save us another $741.00!"

Ted and Annie had just saved six more months of payments and $4,453.00 in interest charges.

His Amortization Schedule now looked like this:

MONTH	PAYMENT	INTEREST	PRINCIPAL	BALANCE
Jan.	~~$900~~	~~$750~~	~~$150~~	~~$149,850~~
Feb.	~~$900~~	~~$749~~	~~$151~~	~~$149,699~~
Mar.	$900	~~$748~~	~~$152~~	~~$149,547~~
Apr.	$900	~~$748~~	~~$152~~	~~$149,395~~
May	$900	~~$747~~	~~$153~~	~~$149,242~~
June	$900	~~$746~~	~~$154~~	~~$149,088~~
July	$900	~~$745~~	~~$155~~	~~$148,933~~
Aug.	$900	~~$745~~	~~$155~~	~~$148,778~~
Sept.	$900	~~$744~~	~~$156~~	~~$148,622~~
Oct.	$900	~~$743~~	~~$157~~	~~$148,465~~
Nov.	$900	~~$742~~	~~$158~~	~~$148,307~~
Dec.	$900	~~$742~~	~~$158~~	~~$148,149~~
Jan.	$900	~~$741~~	~~$159~~	~~$147,990~~
Feb.	$900	~~$741~~	~~$159~~	$147,831

Ted and Annie had now saved a total of $8,938.00 in just two payments, by adding $1,862 to their two payments and making sure their Lender had applied it correctly.

He wrote his note, included instructions on his check, and sent his February payment. However, Ted knew better than to assume his lender would apply the extra amount to his Principal Balance. He called and listened to more music. Ted was simply saving too much money, and the lender was losing too much to assume that the lender would do things the way Ted wanted them done.

After a few months of this, the balances began to match. Ted still calls periodically.

Ted no longer felt trapped in a pit of debt. He had begun his climb out - and he was having fun doing it!

Note: Ted could have simply made double payments or just added extra to his payment each month. If he had made a double payment, his Lender would have treated it as a payment made ahead that Ted would not have to make in the future. He would save very little in interest charges.

Ted's house payment was his largest bill. He needed to keep track of it. He needed to make sure that he was being charged the correct amount of interest.

Ted was so excited. When he received or earned unexpected funds, he knew exactly what he would do with them. Instead of spending the money on something he didn't need, he crossed out another line on his Amortization Schedule. Annie had never paid any attention to bills before. She had been much more interested in charging than paying. Now she was helping Ted.

"Let's make another payment, Ted."

"Let me look and see how much we will need."

"You don't need to. I made a copy of the Schedule. Here. Put this $55 extra on the mortgage this month!"

Ted and Annie are a fictitious couple. Testimonials follow from actual people who took this third step and saved literally years of house payments.

"It Works! We borrowed $48,000 at 10.905% interest for 84 months with $819 payments per month. During the early months, we were able to follow Step Three and pay several principal payments ahead. However, as we got further into the loan, we were able to pay very few principal payments ahead. During the final 2 ½ years, we paid only the payments due. Since we had paid extra in the beginning, our loan was paid in full fourteen months early. We saved a total of $13,111!"

Name Withheld

"We bought a house in June, 1998. Our mortgage was $60,000 at 7.25% interest. Our payments were $409 per month for 30 years. We made extra principal payments whenever we were able, and followed these rules. We sold our house three years later in July, 2001. If we had not followed these steps, our balance would have been $58,007. Instead, our balance was $41,599. We saved $16,408!"

Timothy & Suzanne Courtright

"Our church bought a house adjoining our parking lot on December 6, 1996. We made a large down payment and financed $26,500 at 6% interest. It would take ten years of $294 monthly payments to pay this loan in full. By applying extra principal payments according to these instructions, our loan was paid in just two years! We saved $6,243 in interest charges and 8 years of payments!"

New Life In Christ Church

An Endorsement

"Thank you for affording me the opportunity of advance reading your book on finances. This book is right on target and a must read for anyone wanting to improve their financial standing in life. It is a clear, concise, easy to read, and easy to follow, "how to", in dealing with the financial challenges we all face in life. It is amazing that the financial principals that I apply every day in my practice have been there for all of us, through history, in the Bible. Very well done."

Tim Rehm, "The Financial Doktor"

Tim Rehm is a nationally certified Credit Debt Counselor. Known as "The Financial Doktor," Tim has been providing financial guidance and counsel to families in Baldwin County, Alabama since 1993 through personalized advice and his monthly newspaper column, called **The Second Opinion.**

THE CHIP
By Paul and Carolyn Wilde

Who would imagine that a virus would move us closer to a cashless society? The ***World Health Organization*** (*WHO*) is cautioning the world that cash can transmit bacteria, as it passes hands. The result is a world-wide call for a cashless society. Powerful voices not only want the world to abolish "dirty money", but are also calling for abandoning credit cards and even signatures, in order to prevent another world-paralyzing, economy-crushing pandemic. The coronavirus has moved our world closer to implementing a new world-wide digital currency. ***The Chip*** is an urgent alert of the sinister plans that men are making today. Their aim is to totally control, not only the world of tomorrow… but our brains! Read about cyber-crime; mind control; imaging; transhumanism; artificial intelligence; and quantum computers. Read revealing excerpts from articles that stem from credible sources. Learn why God will be against the new currency to come. What does the chip and its capabilities have to do with God, salvation, and man's eternal destiny? Can a nearly 2,000 year old Bible prophecy be pointing to a chip implanted in humans? If men refuse to have a chip embedded in their hand or forehead, will they forfeit the right to buy and sell?

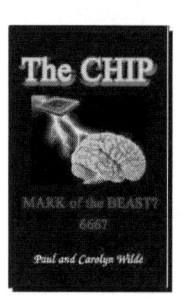

The good news is also included! God has already made the future clear in His Word! He has given wonderful promises to the overcomers!

He has instructed us how to be strong in the Lord, even as the enemies of Christ war against the followers of Christ. He has told us to expect His strength and miracles, even during these trying times.

Soft Cover: 111 Pages
Price: $5.00

WE'VE COME THIS FAR BY FAITH

"I couldn't put this book down!" is the comment heard most often from readers of this inspiring book.

We've Come This Far by Faith will challenge and inspire you.

This book is more than a heart-warming story about the faith journey of a family of ten who learned to trust God. The real story is about our living, faithful, loving God, who loves each of His children and cares about every single one of their needs!

We've Come This Far by Faith is filled with thrilling answers to simple prayers: a loaf of bread when a family is gathered around the breakfast table; a van full of groceries pulling up when cupboards are empty and no one but God has been told there is a desperate need; a mysterious one word message ("Gas") to one of God's listening servants; an anonymous gift of over $220,000 to pay off a church mortgage - all in answer to prayer alone!

We've Come This Far by Faith will encourage you to trust God to both guide and provide for you. The Christian life for every Christian should be an exhilarating faith adventure. We serve a real God who desires to show Himself capable and eager to take wonderful care of His children! This is a book that will build your faith at this critical time in our unstable world. Each of us may soon be facing desperate needs. Each one of us needs to know that we can rely on God to provide our daily necessities!

We've Come This Far By Faith will help you to know that the God of the Bible is still the God of today!

Soft Cover – 286 Pages
Price: $8.00

TORCHBEARERS
By Carolyn Wilde

Dave, an Olympic champion runner, is called by Christ to run with the torch through this sin-blackened world. His race takes him into cities, prisons, skid row missions, campuses, lively churches, dead churches, and city parks. He meets skeptics, invalids, prisoners, alcoholics, homeless children, hardened juveniles, and two very different women.

His look backward through the past 2,000 years brings him face-to-face with valiant runners carrying the torch in every century since John the Baptist began his run.

Dave is shocked to discover:
- Augustine's concern about abortion – in the 5th century!
- Columba's raging temper that littered a field with 5,000 corpses!
- A woman and six men set aflame - for daring to teach their children the Lord's Prayer and Ten Commandments in the English language!

Dave is inspired by:
- John Hus, singing praises to God, while flames devour his body.
- An around-the-clock prayer meeting that lasted 100 years, begun by Count Zinzendorf!
- Villages of American Indians praying and singing entire nights!
- The thrilling conversion of young John Newton, the blasphemous slave trader.
- A sickly woman, who made her way into Tibet by climbing treacherous mountains in raging blizzards, with a murderer as her guide!
- The young man who tapped into the storehouse of God, and became a loving Dad to over 9,500 orphans!

Be challenged along with Dave, as you read actual words from torchbearers' lips, prayers from their hearts, and, in some cases, their dying messages, meticulously gleaned from historical records. Polycarp, Augustine, Patrick, Wyclif, Luther, Tyndale, Wesley, and Finney are all here. Some of the others you will meet are Columba, Waldo, Francke, Annie, Elizabeth, and Savonarola. Our rich Christian heritage will come alive, not just as historical figures, but as real men, women, teenagers, and children who overcame this world, their flesh, and the devil, by the blood of the Lamb, the word of their testimony, and their willingness to both live and die victoriously for their Lord.

Torchbearers is not just another novel with its fictional Dave. **Torchbearers** is not just another history book with its nearly 40 biographies. **Torchbearers** is a call, for it is high-time for all of us to run with the torch. The race is not easy today. But then ... *it never has been*.

COMMENTS FROM READERS:

"One of the best books I have ever read in my lifetime. My life and ministry have not been the same." DWIGHT L. KINMAN, AUTHOR, HOSPITAL CHAPLAIN, & CONFERENCE SPEAKER

"I have shared many passages from **Torchbearers** with my friends and family. I could not put it down! I recommend this book to any person carrying the torch for Jesus who has ever felt alone, rejected, or just in need of a little encouragement." ROSEY BRYAN, WIFE OF ANDY, SOUTHERN BAPTIST EVANGELIST

"... a challenging message and a sharply painted picture of our rich Christian heritage." GULF COAST CHRISTIAN NEWSPAPER

"I was totally in awe! The encouragement one can receive from reading this book is much needed." QUINTON MILLS, EVANGELIST, SONGWRITER

"I constantly use portions of **Torchbearers,** as I minister to the Youth Group in our church." SUZANNE COURTRIGHT, YOUTH DIRECTOR AND TEEN TEACHER

Soft Cover: 432 Pages

SMITTEN SHEPHERDS
By Paul and Carolyn Wilde

Thousands of pastors are leaving the ministry each year. What is behind this exodus from the ministry? Why are so many pastors burned out, emotionally fatigued, physically exhausted, and spiritually discouraged?

SMITTEN SHEPHERDS is dedicated to pastors. It is to the point, straight from the heart, and forged from our over 35 years of pastoring. It is a book written, not to discourage, but to encourage. Pastors and their wives, who have read **SMITTEN SHEPHERDS** are calling and writing to say they have been given extra strength for their race. One evangelist ordered 100 books to encourage pastors, and denominations are ordering 500 and 1,000 books for their discouraged pastors. As our world grows darker, pastors are facing difficult, unceasing challenges.

Pastor, will you be one who will walk away from your call and your church? Or will you continue to fight, keep the faith, and finish your course? Reading these 122 pages may make the difference!

Soft Cover: 122 Pages

TRIUMPHANT THROUGH TRIBULATION
By Paul and Carolyn Wilde

Triumphant Through Tribulation is an in-depth, easy to read book, packed with Scriptures that deal with the following subjects:

- Jesus Is Coming – And Some Claim to Know When!
- Will Christ Return in Phases?
- Why Is Jesus Coming as a Thief In the Night?
- What Is Tribulation? What Is Its Purpose?
- Are Tribulation and Wrath the Same Thing?
- The End-Day Pharaoh
- Portrait of the Antichrist
- The Mark of the Beast
- God's End-Day People
- Will People Be Saved After Christ Returns?
- Voices From the Past and Present

How foolish we would be to ignore the Bible during these closing days of time. God's Word is the **ONE TRUE INSTRUCTION MANUAL** that God, in His mercy and love, has provided for His end-day saints.

Soft Cover – 218 Pages

Paul and Carolyn Wilde have served their wonderful Lord and Savior in full-time ministry for 52 years.

They currently reside in Foley, Alabama, where Paul has served as the founding pastor of *New Life In Christ Church* since 1985.

YOU MAY CONTACT THEM BY:

EMAIL
pcwilde@gulftel.com

THE CHURCH WEB SITE
www.newlifeinchristchurch.net

MAIL
New Life In Christ Church
102 E. Berry Avenue
Foley, AL   36535

Made in the USA
Monee, IL
25 September 2021